Rev. Dr. Marianne Padjan

Award-Winning, Best-Selling Author

Self Empowerment Reset
Forgiveness is for me not them

Legal Disclaimer

Connect with MPowered Voice Publishing
www.MPoweredvoicepublishing.ca

DEDICATION

I dedicate this book and the acts of forgiveness to my father who has taught me more about forgiveness than any other human on earth and to God, who created and gave me the lesson of forgiveness. Forgiveness is not only for me but it's to me as well.

Love and Light

Marianne

FORGIVENESS IS FOR ME NOT THEM

ACKNOWLEDGEMENTS

I would like to take this time to thank God for showing me the way and for always being patient with me especially when it comes to Forgiveness.

Forgiveness is like a muscle that you have to work at the beginning of learning how to forgive. It was tough. It took time and a lot out of me. Now it is second nature when I find that I need to forgive anyone. Typically, if I need to forgive anyone it's usually myself for feeling or thinking the way I do. People are who they are, and they will always do what they do and they will be who they will be. It is not my job to judge them or decide if they're right or wrong. As it is typically something within myself that needs to be addressed and perhaps forgiven.

Life is interesting. Our lessons are mostly irritating at the beginning. And then they become second nature. Just like at the gym you are first building your muscles and then you are maintaining them. The building of them might hurt a little and the maintaining just becomes a habit you master.

Love and Light

Marianne

FORGIVENESS IS FOR ME NOT THEM

TABLE OF CONTENTS

Contents

FOREWORD

Congratulations, Marianne, for addressing this important topic of Forgiveness and bringing together all these authors who have shared their emotional experiences with forgiveness. I can say from personal experience how crucial forgiveness is to mental health.

There have been so many I have had to forgive for the way they treated me, going back to my childhood, through teenage years and onward. Like the authors in this book, I found that resentment added to the anger issues I had to overcome when I first became clean and sober, almost nineteen years ago.

Failing to forgive causes a person to dwell on their past hurts and prevents them from not only enjoying life, but being able to accomplish their personal goals. Once we come to the place where we can see the damage it is doing to ourselves and come to the realization that for our own sake, as well as theirs, we must forgive them, we are in a better position to change our future. Many of the authors described the release and freedom they experienced after they forgave someone for something that had happened maybe years or decades ago.

The title of this book, *"Forgiveness is for me not them,"* illustrates the value that forgiveness brings, not only for the one being forgiven, but primarily to the one doing the forgiving. The authors described their emotional turmoil and even hatred before they forgave and the changes it made in their lives once they forgave, whether or not the person accepted their forgiveness.

Prepare to be affected by the heart-wrenching life accounts and learn from the forgiveness stories of the authors and how forgiveness changed their lives.

Robert J Moore
Featured in Forbes
"Legends of Coaching Award" from Forbes Business Awards
Director of Next Level Coaching

FORGIVENESS IS FOR ME NOT THEM

Introduction

This book took longer to put together than any of my other books to date.

I myself have written my chapter over and over again. If this book were not coming out for another year I would probably change it three more times. As we grow day-by-day, we change our minds over and over again. That is the beauty of life.

Most of the authors in here have taken a great deal of time to build their chapters and their stories. Some have changed them several times some have rethought and rewritten them numerous times.

We have had two eclipses during the time of putting this book together. And if you know anything about the energies that the eclipse brings, you will understand that there have been many, many, fluctuations in emotions, thoughts and therefore physical states as well for most people.

This of course has led to a merry go round of emotions and therefore the authors in this book have gone into the deep dark depths of their soul to give you this book.

With Love and Peace

Marianne

FORGIVENESS IS FOR ME NOT THEM

Forgiveness is Self-Love

Rev. Dr. Marianne Padjan

I wonder what that means to you?

To me it signifies that I have now forgiven this person, who I think did me harm, and taken the responsibility for the fact that I was part of whatever just went down here. For I too was involved and so therefore, I too need to forgive and when I forgive, I'm the one that lightens my own load. I don't lighten it up for other people. I mean if it does help them, that's great. That's the bonus but I'm really doing it for me.

I have now let go of whatever weight comes along with not forgiving this person and I've now made room for all kinds of wonderful things to come into my life. This does not mean that those events have no meaning or do not matter to me. They absolutely do. They just stop weighing me down and that way I can move forward whether it's in business, my personal life, my love life, or my family life.

I realized that some things are just harder to forgive than others. In the grand scheme of things with all the billions of people in this world we're not perfect. We make mistakes and we all require forgiveness. Our thoughts, our feelings, and our actions come mostly from the past. It could be something that has happened or something that hasn't happened. And these are the reasons we are who we are. These are the reasons that we act the way that we do now.

Life is relatively short, and I aim to bring as much light, happiness, and love into my life, which means I too have to exude that energy. Because that is exactly how it works. I too have done things that now, when I remember that when I was younger, I would think to myself, "Oh goodness, what was I thinking?" So, in essence, the perfect place to start with is with yourself. Forgive, forgive, forgive yourself for whatever you may have done or not done in the past We also have done things we wish we had done differently. I know I have. Nobody's perfect, so let's all stop pretending that we are. We're going to probably still make some mistakes even as we get older and smarter.

I find that if we go easier on ourselves, then we have a better chance of going easier on someone else. We can then drop the judgment of others while we're judging ourselves as well. When you think about it, what a big waste of time it is to sit there and pretend we're the judge and jury of the world. Because we're busy judging ourselves, because we felt this way, that way or the other way while we were growing up. Because our father left or because our mother left or because our father was abusive or our mother was abusive or judgmental. Who knows what the reasons are? Maybe our teachers told us things we didn't want to hear; maybe they told us we weren't good enough. Because they were all authoritative figures in our lives; we embraced their opinions as our truth.

I had a very abusive father and a very insecure mother. I also had a teacher, who was a guidance counselor, tell me that I was just too pretty to go and be a psychologist and that I should just stick with retail, because I was too pretty to do all that studying. Today that teacher would land in jail for saying that, or at least, at the very least, lose his job. We go through stages. We learn. We make more mistakes; we go through another stage. We change, we shift, we move. We moved through difficulties. We make new mistakes. We experience new things. We forgive, we make mistakes and so on, and so forth. That part will probably never change, because otherwise we would be robots and what would be the purpose of us being here?

Change is inevitable whether we like it or not. Growth is also inevitable; to what degree and what speed, that is our choice. Within that growth forgiveness is necessary. I must, you must forgive yourself. You must forgive others to be able to move on. Life can be fun and life can be light or it can be heavy. It's always your choice.

Forgive, forgive, forgive.

Rev. Dr. Marianne Padjan

Rev. Dr. Marianne is a 7X international, award winning, bestselling author. Her love of helping entrepreneurs has spanned into a business as an Intuitive/Empowerment Coach, a workshop and Summit Facilitator, Retreat Leader, a DIGITAL TV podcast show host of *MEDITATION MILLIONARE* and a Real Estate agent with EXP Realty Brokerage, where she specializes in working with investors. Definitely it's an eclectic variety that keeps her busy!

Marianne has impacted many lives, both professionally as well as personally. She has guided people form divorce to marriage as well as from bankruptcy to millionaire status.! She also hosts a women's group *MPowered Resilient Women International Mastermind* where a high-end group of women inspire each other to aim even higher. Marianne is now also a senior executive contributor as well as on the expert panel at *Brainz Magazine. MPoweredTalks* is a powerful platform where she helps speakers expand their exposure and credibility!

Marianne Padjan will help you uncover your hidden GREATNESS and show you how to use it. Marianne is a managing director with *APLGO* (The Healthy DNA Candy).

www.MPoweredTalks.com

RELEASE THE ANCHOR

Jose Escobar

Along life's journey, there will be many things that will take a lot out of us but yield tremendous benefit if acted upon. Forgiveness is one of those things. It's not merely just a kind gesture that we offer to others that have done us wrong, but it is a transformative process that in actuality sets us free from the shackles of anger, resentment, and bitterness. In this chapter, my goal is to share some ideas on why it is so critical to forgive in order to be whole.

It can be quite burdensome carrying around such unforgiveness. The image of a beautiful ship tied to its anchor comes to mind. No matter how much effort the ship puts into moving forward, the anchor will hold it back. Holding on to such negativity consumes our energy, tarnishes relationships, and curbs our personal development. Imagine how much progress the ship would make if it cut the anchor! At the end of the day, harboring resentment towards another person is self-defeating and counterproductive to any level of progress.

Naturally, when we forgive someone, we tend to feel like we are doing something good for the other person. However, forgiveness is for you, not them! It has been said, "unforgiveness is like drinking poison and waiting for the other person to die." Can showing grace and forgiveness to the other person be beneficial to them? Yes, of course! But that is not the primary focus. As a Christian, I believe that we can imitate our Heavenly Father when we offer forgiveness just as He offers us forgiveness when we ask for it. In the powerful prayer the "Our Father" it states, "forgive us our trespasses as we forgive those who trespass against us." This bold prayer even links our own forgiveness to how well we forgive others.

Forgiving others is not so much about accepting what they did or condoning their behaviors or actions. Rather, it is about releasing ourselves from the stronghold that unforgiveness can have on our minds and hearts. Additionally, forgiveness adds a renewed sense of peace and joy. Research has shown that embracing forgiveness leads to lower levels of stress, anxiety, and depression. It is in our best interest for the sake of our overall wellbeing to forgive quickly and genuinely.

From my experience, it's easier to forgive people that are more removed from me (*i.e.*, the person who cut me off while driving). It's another thing to forgive those that are closest to me. I've personally had to forgive my parents when they might have said something hurtful and out of pocket. I've had to forgive my wife (shocking, I know) for times that she may have lost her patience with me over something. I've had to forgive my children when they have misbehaved. I've had to forgive close friends over various disagreements. I could continue with countless examples of where forgiveness is required on a regular basis.

Is there a quota for how many times we should forgive someone? In the book of Matthew, the apostle Peter asked Jesus that very question: "Then Peter came to Jesus and asked, *"Lord, how many times shall I forgive my brother or sister who sins against me? Up to seven times?"* Jesus answered, *"I tell you, not seven times, but seventy-seven times.'* (Matthew 18:21-22) This is interpreted as meaning we should not put a limit on how many times we forgive someone.

Forgiveness, just like love, is a choice. It can either break us down and cause us to lose ourselves in the process, or it can empower us to be our best selves and who we are called to be. Refusing to forgive can keep us in a perpetual cycle of hurt and victimhood. If not careful, this can reverberate through generations. Have you ever heard of generational poverty or generational wealth? There is such a thing as generational unforgiveness that can be passed on as a part of a family culture. You have the power to break this cycle. It can continue on with you, or it can end with you. The choice is yours By breaking this cycle, you not only liberate yourself, but you also set up future generations for peace and prosperity.

When we pay close attention and realize that forgiveness is for our own wellbeing, it helps shift the focus from the person who wronged you, to you. Stop waiting for an apology. Stop looking for validation. Stop debating whether you should forgive or not. It's important that you take ownership of your own healing process. As author Bryant McGill stated, "Forgiveness is a gift you give yourself." It's time to stop giving people too much power over you. Don't let other people dictate your happiness, your fulfillment, and your peace of mind.

Here is an anonymous poem that I feel encompasses the essence of forgiveness. Read it carefully and take time to meditate on its message.

In the depths of my soul, a battle once raged,

Where bitterness and anger, their fury engaged.

But then came a whisper, soft yet profound,

A call to release what was tightly wound.

Forgiveness, they said, is a balm for the soul,

A path to freedom, to make oneself whole.

For in forgiving another, we set ourselves free,

From the chains of resentment, we finally flee.

So, I let go of grudges, I let go of pain,

And in that release, I found peace to regain.

No longer a prisoner of hatred's cruel hold,

I stepped into freedom, courageous and bold.

For forgiveness is not weakness, but strength untold,

A beacon of light in a world dark and cold.

It's a gift we give ourselves, a healing embrace,

That fills every corner of our sacred space.

So let us forgive, let us love and let live,

For in forgiveness, true freedom we give.

And as forgiveness flows, like a gentle stream,

We find in its current, our truest dream.

For forgiveness is for me, not them,

A journey of grace, a priceless gem.

So let us forgive, and in forgiveness find,

The peace and the love that heal humankind.

As we encounter opportunities to forgive, let us dive in fully and extend the type of forgiveness that we would like to receive. Remember, forgiveness is a free gift we give to ourselves, and it is a door that we unlock to a much more fulfilling life with limitless possibilities. It is clear that forgiving someone is uncomfortable and sometimes hard, but it is in our discomfort that we grow as individuals. When was the last time you forgave someone wholeheartedly from the depths of your soul? Is there anyone that you are currently holding resentment against? I challenge you to get out a piece of paper and a pen and write some names down. Commit to one name. Reach out to this person and forgive them. Truly forgive them. After all, forgiveness is for you, not them.

Jose Escobar

Jose Escobar, an acclaimed personal development speaker and 14x published author, leads two successful businesses: *The Entrepreneur's Bookshelf* and the *Connected Leaders Academy* that has surpassed over 7-figures in 15 months organically. He engages with entrepreneurs and advanced leaders, collectively reaching over 30 million through presentations and coaching programs. He works with over 400 successful leaders globally.

Jose is a master sales professional. He is happily married with six kids. Discover more about Jose's offerings at:

www.ConnectedLeadersAcademy.com

jose@connectedleadersacademy.com

www.ConnectedLeadersAcademy.com

https://www.linkedin.com/jaesco25

https://www.facebook.com/jaesco25

301-944-4755

Jose Escobar

CEO & Founder - Connected Leaders Academy

CEO - The Entrepreneur's Bookshelf

Mobile: 301-944-4755

Email: jaesco25@gmail.com

Website: www.ConnectedLeadersAcademy.com

www.TheEntrepreneursBookshelf.com

www.WinningTheDayBook.com

FORGIVENESS

Jinna van Vliet

We humans are born as Earthbound citizens who live within a 3D-Duality environment that is controlled and run by the EGO personality. The Ego pattern like the heart is part of our human structure and cannot be removed or ignored. It is part of who we are, human beings on a journey of self-discovery. We were created out of Divine Light and Love itself and must learn the mental and emotional pathways of what is right and what is wrong.

The awareness of the EGO- SELF is mired and anchored within a value system that does not understand the idea of Forgiveness. To be able to have the thought of forgiveness to enter self-awareness, we must first acknowledge the reason for the need to forgive. The reason being the realization that there are right and wrong choices as we traverse the pathways of Life. The Ego-parts will continue to persuade us that doing something bad to others is not wrong but justifiable when we are angry and upset.

Anger usually manifests into an action that our minds accept as a winning situation. When the mind feels that the action was the right choice. it files the thought pattern into a past-forgotten. memory. As we grow older and more mature, life experiences begin to show us a different meaning of life. This is the time when we begin to realize what we have stored in our memory files and the energies of regret and the feelings of sorry for the actions begin to rise to the surface of our awareness.

We begin to face the differences between the shadowy pathways of the EGO persona and the Light lanes of Love. The notion of forgiving anyone is not an easy choice for the human mind and forgiving self is even more challenging for many of us.

It is a private, individual choice of awareness, of beginning to acknowledge what we have done. Once we accept our darkness and choose to be remorseful and ready to repent, the idea of forgiveness rises to the surface of the mind. We begin to realize that asking for forgiveness can only heal our own life for it is the only thing that can bring us peace of mind.

It is the first step towards the spiritual growth of the ME. It is the ME that needed the energies of forgiveness in order to resolve and heal the painful suffering that this Me has chosen to experience in life. Every action of behaviour patterns flows on this earth's realms as waves of light and sound. Our job, our assignment on this Earth is to define and recognize the multiple shades of Light from the black darkness to the gray in between and towards the brilliant Light at the end of the tunnel. The act of forgiveness when wrapped in honesty and truth is the energy bridge that provides the healing lines crossing from the darkness into the light.

Every time we forgive others, we build this bridge within ourselves. This brings the healing balm needed to re-enforce our acceptance that we are part of the Light of Divine Creation. The deepest healing occurs when we begin to forgive our own transgressions and ask others to forgive us.

This emotional choice is not an easy one to make and to act upon because it involves the effort of responsibility to the SELF. The challenging part is to understand that the act of forgiveness does not mean the immediate forgiveness from the people involved in our drama. The true act of forgiveness does not include expectations of outcome. When we make the choice to forgive, we give ourselves permission to shift our very life path into a new direction of peace knowing that we could lose friendships and even family relationships. The following is a poem I wrote to enhance the point of forgiveness.

Harmony of Forgiveness of ME

I forgive my thoughts of the separation of the WE

I release the belief of abandonment of family

I release the emotion of disconnection with the Earth

I choose the evolution of Being with a new rebirth

I see myself reflected in the mirror of truth

I embrace my shadow-self within the human booth

I forgive myself and everything around me

I choose self-Love and just to BE

I ask to be forgiven for each dark thought I had

I forgive myself for every time I am mad

Now I understand that there are no enemies in my life

I was just hurting myself with a dark carving knife

Others in my drama are there for me to learn

Their forgiveness is for my darkness to burn

Myself is the only one who can forgive

Peace is my only choice to live

I choose to create the harmony of creative sound

Within my grounding root the harmony to be bound

I breathe the notes of forgiveness throughout my Tree

I reach out to the awakening that I AM ME

Jinna van Vliet

Shihyin

Shihyin is a channel for the messages of the Goddess Quan Yin. She is a Minister in the Quantum field and in Spiritual Healing processes. She is the published author of *Quan Yin Speaks* and the *Lotus Emerging* series.

Contact info - jinna.vanvliet@gmail.com

EMBRACING FORGIVENESS FOR HEALING, FREEDOM AND DIVINE GRACE

Denise Millett Burkhardt

Forgiveness is a powerful tool that has the potential to transform our lives in profound ways. Oftentimes, we associate forgiveness with letting go of resentment towards others, releasing them from the burden of our anger and hurt. However, what many of us fail to realize is that forgiveness is not just for the benefit of the other person – it is primarily for our own well-being, growth, and inner peace.

When we hold onto grudges, resentments, and anger towards others, we carry a heavy emotional weight that can weigh us down and impact our mental, emotional, and even physical health. The negative energy we hold inside us not only affects our relationships with others but also hinders our own personal growth and happiness. By learning to forgive, we release ourselves from this emotional burden and create space for healing, growth, and transformation in our lives.

Forgiveness is a gift we give ourselves, not the other person. It is an act of self-love and self-compassion that allows us to break free from the cycle of pain and suffering. When we forgive, we let go of the past and open ourselves up to new possibilities and opportunities for growth and happiness.

Moreover, holding onto anger and resentment towards others only perpetuates our own suffering. It keeps us stuck in a negative cycle of blame, victimhood, and disempowerment. By choosing to forgive, we take back our power and reclaim control over our own lives. We no longer allow the actions of others to dictate our emotional state or determine our happiness.

Forgiveness is also a key component of personal growth and spiritual development. It requires us to confront our own vulnerabilities, fears, and insecurities, and to cultivate empathy, understanding, and compassion towards ourselves and others. Through the act of forgiveness, we not only heal our past wounds but also create a foundation for healthier and more fulfilling relationships in the future.

In addition to forgiving others, it is essential to seek forgiveness from a higher power, from God or the divine source that we believe in. As human beings, we are imperfect and prone to making mistakes. Seeking forgiveness from a higher power allows us to acknowledge our faults and shortcomings, and to humbly ask for divine grace and mercy to cleanse our souls and guide us on the path of righteousness.

When we seek forgiveness from God, we open ourselves up to receiving divine love, healing, and guidance. We surrender our egos, pride, and embrace humility and gratitude in the presence of the divine. By seeking forgiveness from God, we acknowledge our interconnectedness with the universe and align ourselves with the higher purpose and plan that is greater than ourselves.

In essence, forgiveness is a deeply personal journey that begins and ends with ourselves, while also encompassing our relationship with the divine. It is a path towards self-discovery, self-acceptance, and self-transformation, guided by the divine grace and love that flows through us and connects us to all of creation.

By embracing forgiveness for ourselves and seeking forgiveness from God, we free ourselves from the shackles of the past and step into a brighter, more empowered future filled with love, joy, and peace. Forgiveness is a sacred act of self-care, divine grace, and spiritual growth that allows us to heal, grow, and flourish in harmony with ourselves and the universe.

So, remember, forgiveness is not just for someone else – it is for you and for your connection with the divine. Embrace forgiveness as a sacred act of self-care and divine grace, and watch as it transforms your life in ways you never thought possible, bringing you closer to inner peace, spiritual fulfillment, and divine love.

Denise Millett Burkhardt

Denise Millett Burkhardt was born and raised in Brooklyn, New York, and received a congressional award for her invaluable service to the community. She also received the "Producer's Award", from the Mayor of Los Angeles for being multicultural and making the city a better place to live and work.

The youngest woman ever to own an OTT Network, Denise has given away over 12 million charitable dollars of airtime on 14 networks for 5 years. She has built out 18 TV networks, and now has a platform, Traverse TV, that will be a basis for positive reinforcement through music, entertainment, health, nutrition, education and information, all rated PG-14, reaching a global audience. She is working on a project to house 30-40,000 homeless Veterans and end their homeless situation by the year 2030 by duplicating the program in every State.

Very soon, she will be rolling out a K-12 Global Educational Program that will pay students in crypto currency to learn and get an overall better education through Satellite Delivery. She will also be launching a Worldwide Tele-Medicine Platform through Satellite Delivery that will provide unlimited options for medical care.

MOM'S APPLE PIE = FORGIVENESS
Lisa Charles

Dedicated to: Mrs. LaVerne Millicent Russell (My mother, a high school debate champion and Howard University Thespian, dedicated her life to enriching and transforming the lives of our youth through her lifelong commitment as a social worker)

The kitchen was bathed in warm, golden light, and the sweet scent of apples and cinnamon hung in the air. I stood by the kitchen table, a young and curious observer, as my Mom, LaVerne Millicent Russell, embarked on her sacred ritual – making her renowned apple pie. Her hands moved with a grace born of countless pie-making sessions, and her voice, soothing and confident, filled the room. My Mom's kitchen was a place of warmth and togetherness. It was the heart of our home, and her apple pies symbolized her love.

She often said, "A pie made with love tastes better," I couldn't agree more. Her pie-making was an art form, and every step was performed with intention and care. "See Lisa," my Mom would say, her eyes twinkling as she held up a perfect Granny Smith apple. "You want apples that are just a bit tart, not overly sweet. They'll balance the flavors beautifully." I nodded, hanging onto her every word. She continued, her hands expertly peeling the apples, the skins curling away like ribbons. "And the flavor," she continued, her tone gentle. "The key to the pie's flavor is the delicate mixture of brown sugar, cinnamon, and butter, just like this." She demonstrated, her fingers gently massaging the sweet butter mixture into each slice of apple. "And don't forget a pinch of nutmeg for that perfect balance."

As I watched her, I realized that my Mom's apple pie was more than a delicious dessert. It was a labor of love, a meticulous process that she approached with care and attention to detail. Her explanations were not just about making a pie; they were lessons in patience, love, and craftsmanship.

Although they seem like an unlikely pair, apple pie, and forgiveness have more in common than you might think. Both can be part of our shared human experience, invoking comfort, warmth, and love. With both, there is an intricate process that demands patience and care. And just as my Mom's pie was a symbol of love, forgiveness too is rooted in the profound need for love and healing.

The benefits of forgiveness are undeniable, yet its execution often eludes us. We might long for the emotional release that only forgiveness gives, but not everyone knows how to navigate the process. Much like baking my Mom's delectable pie, forgiveness requires understanding the ingredients and the steps involved. Think about it. When pie-making, you start with raw ingredients – spices, butter, apples, sugar. They're like the raw emotions we begin with when seeking forgiveness. When we are wronged or hurt, our raw emotions of anger, sadness, and resentment may overwhelm our spirit. Just as my Mom carefully selected each ingredient necessary for the pie, we must acknowledge and understand those negative emotions when we seek forgiveness.

The First Step in both processes is acknowledging those raw ingredients. Just as my Mom chose the suitable apples, we must recognize our pain for forgiveness. It can be challenging, as selecting the perfect apples can often be tricky. Sometimes, we want to ignore the pain, but my Mom always said, "You can't make a good pie with bad apples." In other words, you can't find true forgiveness without acknowledging the hurt.

The Second Step is to build. My Mom would spend significant time mixing the apples with sugar, cinnamon, a touch of nutmeg, and vanilla. It was a blend that had been perfected over generations and always produced the most amazing flavor. She would ensure each apple slice was coated entirely with this scrumptious mixture.

It took time. It required loving persistence. As a pie's filling needs time to marinate, forgiveness involves time and patience. You can't force it. You need to let the emotions settle, just like the flavors needed to combine. It was a delicate balance, and impatience could lead to the pie's loss of flavor or a lack of true forgiveness and its resulting freedom.

For pie-making and forgiveness, there is an underlying focus on achieving the best result. In pie-making, it was a delectable dessert; in forgiveness, it is emotional, mental, and spiritual reconciliation. The goal of forgiveness is to let go of negative emotions, just as my Mom let go of any imperfections in her pies. The pie-making process demanded precision and attention to detail. The apples had to be sliced just right, not too thick, or thin. The spices had to be measured accurately. And the oven had to be preheated to the perfect temperature. It was a symphony of flavors and textures, each element carefully considered to create the ultimate pie. It's the foundation upon which everything else is built. With a strong foundation, my Mom understood that the pie would thrive.

Similarly, forgiveness requires us to pay attention to the details of our emotions. We must not only acknowledge the hurt but also our own role in the situation. It's about understanding the nuances of each life event and finding a way to let go of anger and resentment. It is a process that builds character, strengthens compassion, goodness, kindness, and generosity, forming the foundation for forgiveness. It's a journey of self-discovery and understanding that enables us to envision a life beyond pain. With a strong character, forgiveness will be attainable.

Just as my Mom's pies were a result of meticulous preparation, forgiveness is the result of careful self-reflection and understanding Patience is vital as we allow the pain to reveal itself over time, paving the way for multi-dimensional healing.

Step 3: Letting go– We must let go of the hurt and anger towards ourselves or others. We must release lingering grudges and negative feelings and move forward with peace and acceptance. While this may be difficult, there is no forgiveness without letting go. But with the strength of character and acknowledgment of the truth, forgiveness and its countless benefits are within your grasp. Letting go of anger and resentment is like the final step in baking the pie to perfection. It's the moment when you take the pie out of the oven, and it's golden brown and fragrant. It's an acceptance of the pie, whatever the outcome, understanding that it results from careful preparation and patience.

And just as a well-baked pie is a joy to behold and delectable to taste, forgiveness brings a sense of peace and freedom that is truly beautiful. A clear mind and focused heart are essential for achieving the best results in pie-making and forgiveness. Just as my Mom's kitchen was a place of love and intention, forgiveness required us to approach it with love and intention.

In conclusion, just as my Mom's apple pie-making was an act of love, forgiveness is an expression of love – love for oneself and others. The "why" behind both endeavors is to create something beautiful, whether a delicious pie or a harmonious relationship. Like a perfect pie, true forgiveness brings joy, healing, and the promise of a better future.

As I reflect on those moments in my Mom's kitchen, watching her create magic with apples and spices, I realize that forgiveness is a bit like pie-making. It requires time, patience, and a loving touch. And just as my Mom's pies brought our family closer together, forgiveness can mend relationships and bring peace to our hearts.

So, the next time you need to forgive, remember the lessons from my Mom's apple pies.

Take the time to acknowledge the hurt, build the inner character needed for forgiveness, and let go of anger and resentment. Doing so will create something beautiful – not just a perfect pie but a life filled with love, compassion, and true forgiveness. And just like my Mom's pies, it will be a recipe for a life well-lived.

Lisa Charles

Lisa is an award-winning Keynote Speaker and Best-Selling Author of "*Yes! Commit Do Live*" – a book centered on training people to tap into the Brain-Body connection enabling them to embrace any passion and desire and turn it into tangible results.

Lisa is also the CEO of *Embrace Your Fitness, LLC*, a wellness consultancy driven to bring innovative, creative, and effective Wellness programs to individuals, corporations, and organizations.

After serving as a federal prosecutor and singer/actress, Lisa found a passion for wellness as a Coach and Trainer after successfully shedding 77 lbs without dieting using her signature 'Commit. Do. Live' strategy. She then served as the Fitness/Wellness Research Coordinator for the Rutgers University Aging & Brain Health Alliance.

Now, as a Brain, Body, and Belief Alignment Expert, Lisa specializes in Sleep management and Breathing techniques empowering corporate employees and individuals to let go of their limiting beliefs, find their creativity, embrace who they are, and break through any age-limiting barriers, by allowing them to experience wellness from her top/down, inside/out approach.

She is the co-creator of *Reinventing the Women Mastery* group and the provider of international retreats the help individuals experience the Age Defying Life by releasing stress, renewing energy, restoring sleep, while gaining the mental clarity to live the life of your dreams.

Contact Lisa:

lisa@YesCoachLisa.com

www.YesCoachLisa.com

https://www.linkedin.com/in/embraceyourfitness/

https://www.facebook.com/yescoachlisa/

https://www.bsaprinc.com/speakers-bureau

(973) 704-2214

Forgiveness – As a Young Girl, Daughter and Wife

Tammy Williams

Have you heard the words, *"Honesty is a lonely word"*? Well, I beg to differ — FORGIVENESS is. We all know too well that many have a difficult time with forgiving hence, the number of losses of friendships, dissolved marriages, breakdowns in business relationships, estranged relationships with family members and not communicating with our neighbors. Heck, we may have even heard of people losing or quitting a job or firing a client.

Speaking as a daughter with a living birth father with whom I have no relationship with, by his choice, as a wife of 25 years, mom of three, daughter, sister, and niece, the list is long. I have plenty of first-hand experience with the damaging power that lies in not forgiving.

It's feeling stuck not understanding why things are not going the way you have planned; noticing the instructions that you are following aren't working out. It brings about mixed emotions: anxiety, anger and hurt.

Turning back the pages in a calendar, I recall a simple game of Red Rover Red Rover. I'm dating myself here, lol, and not being the first pick by my closest friend. I remember being upset to the point where I no longer wanted to be her friend because others laughed and poked fun at me that I wasn't the first pick by my dearest and closest friend. This was a friend that was always at my house for dinners, movie-watching, games, you name it. After that day, I cut off the friendship without an explanation. It wasn't until years later when we met up again, in my late teens, that time had softened my heart and we began a friendship again.

We had a great conversation to clear the air which gave us both a good understanding of what had really happened. I felt lighter and realized that letting bygones be bygones was a part of forgiving and that I was still alive. Contrary to what I thought, it didn't kill me. This was such immature thinking on my part, but hey I grew from it. I learned to communicate my feelings because the person may not have had any intention of hurting the other person and then lose years not being friends anymore.

As I began to get a softer heart and read more, I learned that forgiveness was really for me not for those I felt hurt by. I noticed I was blossoming, becoming more extroverted, more patient and not holding a mental image of how I wanted people to treat me, but rather just let them be who they were. There was a shift in my grades at school from some C-c's to B's, my athleticism improved, and I was chosen as Captain of some teams. My confidence soared. I began trying out /signing up for everything. There was something freeing and light about it. At that age, I didn't know what was taking place I just knew that I felt different.

It was around that time that my brother and I both realized that this man who was our birth father was really just going to continue his great life choosing not to acknowledging us. I mean, really how could this birth father continue on with his life, raising three other children and not acknowledge us?

~ 26 ~

This came with a lot of tears, confusion, uncertainty, anger, and this heavy feeling - like a 50 lb bag of potatoes - that I felt I was carrying for years. I didn't want to forgive him; to me he didn't deserve it. Although my mom married a wonderful man that I called daddy, who had given me love, attention and a solid foundation and instilled that I mattered, I was kind of bitter and angry. I guess I wasn't ready to forgive him.

You see, I saw my mom raise three children on her own and become a widow while in the third trimester of her pregnancy and be full of joy, not bitterness. Thankfully, over time, it rubbed off on me. It took me into my 30's as mom to forgive him which fueled me to focus on how I wanted my life to be. It gave me courage to do things I never intended on doing like going 100% commission at a job I had for a little over 6 years. It was FREEING to the bones. I could think more clearly, sleep better, I had more energy etc., the list is long. This would be my first time of being aware of the power of forgiveness!

Thank God for my mother and the many childhood lessons through Sunday school. I would play in my mind over and over one that still remains in my heart and is a part of my daily life actions, "Treat others as I would like to be treated."

Fast forward to being a wife of 25 years with some ups and downs, I can say that forgiveness has to be right up there with the word LOVE. Forgiveness in abundance or lack thereof can make or break a marriage. Every celebratory year of marriage is also a way of saying I am sorry, I forgive you, we made it. Sometimes we are quicker to forgive a stranger or someone we don't love or share a life with than the ones we truly love. You won't know which way you will sway unless you have the right mindset about self-love. What love is to you as well as knowing forgiveness doesn't mean you have to feel stuck there. With the right help and support you can choose YOU, lay down the law and/ or leave.

This is not easy to do but rewarding over time. Forgiveness becomes something you value along with God or whatever you feel your source is. I'm not saying not to have a deal breaker if you so desire, but just know that forgiveness may change everything and without it, things will remain the same. While many may feel they are living without forgiving, not forgiving literally blocks your blessings. While choosing to carry the energy that comes with not forgiving the individual(s) may have forgotten they hurt or betrayed you, or don't even know, or care and are living it up. All the while, it shrinks our being like a blueberry that is left out of the fridge for days because it is out of its element like us humans.

Forgiveness is the true path to living on purpose that allows us to add intention to our lives. It's like a book or movie that never gets old, no race or gender, it just is forgiveness. Feeling stuck, not sleeping well, having anxiety and no real focus can all be related to not forgiving.

What really helped to forgive:

- was holding forgiveness in a higher regard

- not holding onto grudges

- making peace with the situation or person

- placing the words self-love next to forgive

- being aware of my feelings

- not being hard on myself

- not listening to others' opinions

- knowing it's related to better health *.i.e.,* better sleep, moods and focus,

LETTING GO AND LETTING GOD!

Tammy Williams

Tammy Williams is a wife, mom of three, still makes her husbands lunch, a 5x International Best-Selling Author, Entrepreneur with over 15 years in marketing and sales experience.

She has a passion for helping break the inequities that women have been faced with for centuries hence her collaboration as an Advisory Board Member with *Camera's For Girl's*, a registered Charity.

She is the Founder of *Women, Champagne and Real Estate* and *CryptoSmart Chicks*. A firm believer that your health is wealth has led to her being a Health Advocate with APLGO. She has worked in the Diabetes and Auyervada Health sectors as well. She also believes we all can give and started a *Walk a Mile in Her Shoes* campaign several years ago that has collected over 400 pairs of ladies new and gently worn footwear which have been donated to various places in Durham region.

https://womenchampagneandrealestate<https://womenchamp agneandrealestate/>.com
tammy@womenchampagneandrealestate.com<mailto:tammy @womenchampagneandrealestate.com>

She can be found on social media:

Facebook Women, Champagne and Realestate

https://www.facebook.com/groups/womenchampagnerealesta te/?ref=share

Instagram

tammy_unlimited

champagnelivingbytammy

LinkedIn https://www.linkedin.com/mwlite/in/tammy-williams-59b098265

RECLAIMING POWER THROUGH FORGIVENESS

Yara N. Ortiz

Ephesians 4:32 "And be kind to one another, tenderhearted, forgiving one another, even as God in Christ forgave you."

For almost fifteen years, I lived in a cage. Not a physical one with bars and locks, but a cage, nonetheless. It was constructed of manipulation, control, and fear, built by the hands of the man I once thought I loved. He portrayed himself as charismatic, charming, and appeared to be the perfect partner. But behind closed doors, he was an entirely different person. He turned out to be a narcissistic and manipulative man who thrived on power and control. So much so, that he made it his business to isolate me from my friends and family, wanting me to depend entirely on him. In group settings, he dictated when I could speak and monitored my interactions, to ensure I didn't go "out of his line". And his weapon to make sure I didn't go out of line was to instill fear. he succeeded, I lived in constant fear of his anger that I was living like a prisoner in my own life.

It took me years to muster the courage to break free from his grasp. The decision to leave was not an easy one - I knew that I was risking everything, including the safety of my son and myself. But I also knew that I couldn't continue living in the shadow of his control any longer. When I finally walked out; it was one of the scariest days of my life. Every step felt like a leap into the unknown, fearing his retaliation. The day I walked out the door marked the beginning of a new chapter, but the fear lingered, haunting me as I navigated life as a single parent.

In the aftermath of leaving, I knew that I had to find a way to forgive him. Not for his sake, but for mine. I didn't want to carry the weight of anger and bitterness with me for the rest of my life and much less pass that on to my son. I wanted peace, closure, and the chance to start fresh. But forgiveness wasn't easy. It wasn't a one-time decision, but a daily struggle, a conscious effort to let go of the pain and resentment that had taken root in my heart. I turned to my faith, seeking relief and guidance in prayer, asking God to help me find the strength to forgive. It was a long and arduous journey, filled with setbacks and struggles.

There were days when the hurt felt fresh, when the wounds he had inflicted upon me seemed impossible to heal. But I refused to give up. I refused to let him continue to hold any power over me. Taking one step at a time, and one day at a time I learned to recognize the triggers that threatened to pull me back into the darkness, and I found ways to counteract them, to reclaim my sense of self-worth and dignity. I began to feel the burden of unforgiveness lifting from my shoulders.

Fast forward to today; I can say with certainty that I have forgiven this man. Not because he deserves it, but because I deserve peace. I deserve to live my life free from the shackles of resentment and anger. Though scars remain, I no longer allow them to define me. I have learned to let go of the past, to focus on the present and the future. I have rediscovered and love myself again and believe in my own strength and resilience.

The journey to forgiveness was long and difficult, but it was worth it. I carry with me the lessons I've learned and the wisdom I've gained, realizing that I am stronger than I ever thought possible, capable of overcoming even the darkest of trials. Though the road ahead may still be uncertain, I walk it with confidence, knowing that I am free from the cage that once held me captive, free to live my life on my own terms, free to forgive and to love again. I am grateful for the journey that has brought me to this moment, and I am excited for the adventures that lie ahead. With forgiveness in my heart and hope in my soul, I step boldly into the future, ready to embrace whatever comes my way.

The journey to freedom and forgiveness didn't just end with the physical departure from this man's oppressive grasp. It was an ongoing process, a daily commitment to reclaiming my sense of self and rebuilding my life on my terms. Along the way, I discovered the power of self-care and self-compassion. I learned to prioritize my own well-being and to treat myself with kindness and gentleness. Surrounding myself with supportive friends and family also played a crucial role in my healing journey. Their love and encouragement reminded me that I was not alone and that I was worthy of happiness and fulfillment.

But perhaps the most transformative aspect of my journey was learning to forgive myself. For years, I carried the weight of guilt and shame for allowing myself to stay in an abusive relationship. I blamed myself for not leaving sooner, for not being strong enough to break free from David's control. However, I've come to realize that I was doing the best I could with the resources and knowledge available to me at the time. I showed immense courage and resilience in eventually breaking free and embarking on the path to healing.

As I reflect on my journey, I am filled with gratitude for the growth and transformation it has brought into my life. While the scars of the past may still linger, they serve as reminders of my strength and resilience. I no longer define myself by the pain and suffering I endured but by the courage and resilience that carried me through it. I am a survivor, not a victim, and I am empowered to create the life I deserve.

In forgiving David, I reclaimed my power and my freedom. I released the hold his actions had over me and liberated myself from the chains of resentment and bitterness. Forgiveness was not about excusing or condoning his behavior but about freeing myself from the burden of carrying hatred and anger in my heart. It allowed me to move forward with my life, unencumbered by the weight of the past, and to embrace the present with hope and optimism.

Today, I stand tall and proud, a testament to the strength of the human spirit and the transformative power of forgiveness. While the journey was long and arduous, it was worth every step. I am grateful for the lessons learned, the growth experienced, and the freedom gained. As I look to the future, I do so with a renewed sense of purpose and a deep-seated belief in my ability to overcome any obstacle that comes my way. With forgiveness in my heart and hope in my soul, I step boldly into the unknown, ready to embrace whatever the future holds.

Yara N. Ortiz

Yara N. Ortiz is the owner of *Bookkeeping Consulting Services*.She is a successful financial consultant who's helped many nonprofit organizations and small businesses increase their cash flow by structuring their financial management systems.

Yara is a driven individual who holds a Bachelor's degree in Accounting. With 15 years of experience in financial management for nonprofits, she deeply understands their challenges. Yara's unique perspective in her work is shaped by her lived experiences and upbringing in Puerto Rico & the Bronx, NY. Before establishing her company, she served as the finance director of a charter school in her community.

Yara is passionate about empowering nonprofit leaders with essential financial knowledge and helping them develop robust systems. While nonprofits are Yara's area of specialized expertise, she extends her invaluable services to encompass small businesses and personal financial planning for individuals. When she's not hard at work for her clients, Yara treasures spending time with her son, exploring the wonders of nature, enjoying Zumba sessions, or immersing herself in the pages of a captivating book.

Contact Yara:

Email: info@bookkeepingcs.com
Website: bookkeepingcs.com
Linktree: https://linktr.ee/yaraortiz

FORGIVENESS IS FOR ME

Albert Lacoursiere

I want to share some of my thoughts that have stemmed from conversations I've had with friends and family about a variety of situations or experiences. I would bet that others have had similar experiences and a range of other sentiments or responses.

Sometimes good intentions and good ideas lead to disaster. There could be a situation where somebody loaned a significant amount of money or borrowed something of great value from somebody they trusted with the promise of getting it back. Instead of getting the money or the item back, they were instead told that it was lost and unable to be returned. An apology and explanation may be given but the bottom line is that they felt a bit taken or let down by somebody they trusted. The initial reaction could be a feeling of confusion or surprise that something like this could have happened.

Then maybe anger, disappointment, frustration and probably even anxiety set in about what will happen moving forward without this thing of importance. Some of these feelings could be directed at the person responsible for the loss or perhaps towards the situation or cause of the loss. How could they let this happen after an agreement or promise was made about the safe care and return of this possession?

Will they let this misfortune permanently shape the future relationship with the individual at fault? Money or items can be regained for the most part. Although this situation of loss might make them reconsider loaning or borrowing in the future, they may be able to see past the fault or mistake and remain amicable.

Business operators constantly face decisions; some that aren't very important but others that are pretty major. Many decisions are made that have ended up being the wrong one and resulted in very negative outcomes and feel very catastrophic. This can feel devastating to the individual and to their business partners.

This is one responsibility of a business operator. The partners know and should understand that you can't win them all. Some days there are victories and you go home at the end of the day energized and excited for the next opportunity. Other days it can be quite the opposite. You end the day feeling a bit defeated and replay the mistake in your head. It's important to learn lessons from mistakes, and if you are going to keep anything from a fault, let it be the lesson.

Find a healthy way of dealing with the aftermath. Perhaps this means talking with your business partners about what happened and why. Identify what the challenge was and what could have been done differently. Try to remember why it was that you made that decision. Perhaps it was a calculated risk and was in fact the right decision.

There will be more decisions to make tomorrow so try to give yourself a bit of a break because you will have more opportunities tomorrow. From a different perspective, it could be that it was your business partner who made the mistake and is now dealing with the psychological consequences of their actions. Nobody wants to screw up. Go easy on them. You need them to bring a positive energy to the workplace tomorrow in order to keep things moving forward towards success.

Sometimes people hurt each other. Forgiveness is important but sometimes it runs out. There could be a scenario or situation where a person is being hurt, mistreated, or abused, through the words or actions of somebody over and over again.

Although they can be given the benefit of the doubt that again it was unintentional, perhaps the person doing these things has no self awareness, or perhaps they are fully aware of what they are doing. It may be a tough choice but it may be important to close the door on forgiveness towards this person and instead accept the fact that your future is not going to improve if you allow this dynamic to continue. This could be the time to distant yourself from that person, and accept things for how they are and that this person's actions are characteristic of them and nothing to do with you. It could be uncomfortable when thinking about creating the gap between you and this other person, but you need to consider your own wellness first.

You may have regrets and there will perhaps be consequences but don't forget the reasons. If you are leaving a toxic relationship and there are children involved, then it can get even more complicated. Depending on the situation, you may continue to be somehow tied to this person if you let's say share custody with them and are required to continue to communicate with them for things concerning the kids.

Unfortunately, this can sometimes be enough of a tie to each other for hurtful words or actions to continue. In a situation like this, forgiveness maybe doesn't come into play. You are no longer accepting the wrongdoings dealt you on a emotional level, then slapping a forgiveness bandage on them because you want to believe that it was unintentional. You already know that the person causing this harm either has no self awareness or is completely aware of what they are doing. You are dismissing the insignificant and unimportant hurtful actions or words because you understand the source from which they are produced.

This person no longer has control over you and it can be very empowering once you grasp this concept and focus on your own awareness and actions when you are around them and around others. You don't always need to forgive others for their ongoing actions but if you must, accept that they are who they are and that it's no longer your concern.

Conclusion

With 40 years of experience as being human, I have made my fair share of mistakes and there are more to come. I have said and done things that have caused frustration, anger, disappointment to others and to myself. I have used poor judgment and placed myself into undesirable predicaments. I can't undo these things, but I try to make things right. Hope for forgiveness from those you have hurt and try to make more mindful choices in the future. Forgive yourself for things you feel you did wrong.

Acknowledge faults but don't forget to move on with your life by instead remaining too busy for dwelling on mistakes or results of misjudgment. We are only human.

Albert Lacoursiere

Albert grew up in rural Saskatchewan with three siblings. Albert is very fortunate and grateful that his parents not only worked extremely hard to provide for their four children, but that they also focused on doing things as a family. Having children of his own within non-traditional family dynamics, Albert has had frustrating and emotional experiences of dealing with custodial matters within Canada's flawed family law system.

With support from family, friends, and personal development coaches, Albert worked his way through many challenges. Albert understands that the best tools to move forward are to practice having a positive state of mind to accept certain things and to better direct his focus and energy towards things that are productive and constructive.

Learning to accept unfavorable things along the way has been crucial to his success and development to where he is now.

Farm life offered Albert many unique skills and opportunities and he developed a mindset of having interest in diversity. While continuing to be active with farming, Albert also enjoys studying real estate investing, learning about crypto currencies, continuing personal development, practicing creative writing, taking motorcycle trips, enjoying anything outdoors in a variety of other ways and spending time with his family and kids.

FORGIVENESS BENEFITS

Linda McBee

Forgiveness was a hard word for me to comprehend when I was young, but I learned to embrace it, freeing and releasing the subconscious anxiety that I didn't know was there.

The Bible teaches that unselfish love is the basis for forgiveness, since "*it keeps no record of wrongs*" (1 Corinthians 13:5). Forgiving others means letting go of resentment and giving up any claim to be compensated for the hurt or loss we have suffered.

I am thankful that God orchestrated people in my life to give me wisdom to educate me about what forgiveness means. I didn't see much as an example of what this truly meant, but heard people say it. When trauma is a part of your story, forgiveness seems insurmountable. Trauma can come in many ways. What is trauma and how can it affect your life and forgiveness?

Growing up in church was my saving grace. I heard this often to forgive others but struggled to wrap my head around it and from a heartfelt understanding of the process of how to do it. No one knew the secrets happening in my home. I would say to myself, "That is easy for you to say and do." No one knew what was happening in my life and the pain I was in. "You didn't lose your mom before you started school," "or have a mom figure that was abusing you and threatened you if you said something."

This caused me to be bitter and forgiving her was way out of the question or at least at that moment. God had orchestrated the people to be in my life to teach me how important forgiveness would be to be a healthy adult. If you haven't forgiven as the definition says it leads to long-term mental disorders caused by past anxiety.

I am grateful for a doctor that took a real interest in me and my health. I was about 11 years old, and he educated me about sugar and food since at the time I was overweight by more than 60 pounds. I know that the education I received about forgiveness from my church and how food and nutrition were affecting my body, is why I continue to help people understand what is happening in our lives on an emotional level majorly affects our health.

People want to push under the rug what is happening to them and then do not understand why they have the health issues they have including their weight, heart issues, high blood pressure, and the list goes on. Society has made it easy to take a pill and eliminate the disorder, but that just buries the pain more, and now they have side effects to the medication that they were given for the original issue.

Unresolved anger that is buried for years can affect your heart rate, blood pressure, and natural defenses. Health is wealth! When you don't have your health, life is very limited in offerings in the energy you have. The changes increase the risk of hopelessness, heart disease, and diabetes, among other health problems. Diabetes is what I was going through before I started working with the doctor who helped to educate me about food, especially sugar.

It didn't happen overnight, but the mindset helped me work emotionally on what was happening and focus on good healthy foods along with his program that helped me lose the extra weight over the next two years. The emotional trauma was one of the reasons I was out of control with eating. After getting my sugar addiction under control, I could begin to not only forgive others but finally myself.

This took some time, but the more I forgave others and myself, the fewer health issues I experienced. Forgiveness has been something I was encouraged to do, and when I embraced it, it was life-changing! I had never thought about forgiving myself or realizing things that happened created pictures in my conscious and subconscious mind that affected me. Reframing pictures in my brain gave me a different visual and helped me to let go of more of the pain in myself to put positive pictures now.

My forgiveness process continued while I pushed through what allowed me to release the pain that was causing my health problems from my childhood. The doctor that started to work with me when I was young helped me understand what I was eating and gave me the confidence I needed to develop.

This process has been constant and today I love to help people with their health. One little trick I realized is that the more confident I got, the more I forgave myself and others. Forgiveness is something I look at sometimes a few times a day. How did I handle something? Did I say something I shouldn't have? Could I have handled the situation better?

I do something called a self-inventory a few times a week or sometimes daily. It is acting when something happens that you get upset about or causes anger. Three aspects of forgiveness are critical to your health and well-being! They are in order to forgive others; we need forgiveness from others and to forgive ourselves.

In forgiving others, it might be in person, through a letter that you send to them, or one that is written but is not shared with the person you wrote about but a support person. You might do this with an ex-spouse. That it is you who needs to get it on paper and release the pain. I did this with my dad's wife, who had a mental health issue and would not have understood.

I talked to my dad since he was too far away and wanted to reconnect immediately on a deeper level. If you have been through any twelve-step programs this advice would be familiar to you.

I would be happy to help you forgive either yourself or someone else to free you from the stress and anxiety of past pain. Forgiveness is a very powerful process, both an internal and external force that is life-changing!

Do it TODAY!

Linda BcBee

Helping people with their health and navigating life has become Linda's passion since being a teen, both personally and professionally, working with businesses alongside having her own. Cooking exceptional food became her expression. Keeping it simple with spices is her passion.

Growing up in a garden, eating fresh vegetables, and learning to compost to restore the nutrients in the soil is critical. Linda believes giving soil extra nutrients is like taking herbs and botanicals to boost the food we eat. She teaches through experience and explains how trying to eliminate gluten and other chemicals was a good start, and sourcing herbs and additional nutrients to help her cells heal has been a journey.

Autoimmune issues are something she's been battling since she was young. Over time they snowballed into being diagnosed with neurological Lyme disease.

Finding herbs and phytonutrients her body didn't reject was critical in the search for better health. Linda was fortunate to be introduced to a full line of botanicals a few years ago that are lozenges and have been game-changers.

One of them addresses gut issues and eliminating parasites, which was a lifesaver for her journey, ridding her of the brain fog, being sick every time she ate, and increasing her energy level to get back to life again.

Another botanical was for prework and stamina. The latest addresses visceral fat, which is a silent killer, and high in B vitamins. This has been critical since she doesn't assimilate Vitamin B and now can because of the delivery system.

She is working with coaches, weight loss centers, wellness centers, practitioners, and mental health centers, directing them around health and loving their inner child to be their best version of themselves.

She also is marketing additional products and services to help businesses with solutions and consistent revenue streams.

She'd love to cheer you on your business journey.

Please reach out to her at linktr.ee/LindaMcBee

SETTING BOUNDARIES AND FORGIVENESS: A PERSONAL JOURNEY

Julia Flynn Werre

Setting boundaries has never been very easy for me. In fact, most of the time, I could never set any boundaries. This goes all the way back to when I was a kid. Back in those days, I was in Catholic school, and we were taught things like being a Good Samaritan, speaking when spoken to, and that children are to be seen and not heard. Because of that, I was in a world of boundaries set by other people and adults and quickly became a people pleaser. I somehow got the message that it was my job as a human being to please other people, to be a good girl, and to follow the rules. Well, that's good for a child. It's not good for an adult woman who runs her own business and who is an entrepreneur through and through.

The Influence of the Golden Rule and the Good Samaritan

The Golden Rule is a moral principle found in many cultures and religions, commonly stated as, "*Do unto others as you would have them do unto you.*" In Catholic school, this was emphasized as the foundation of ethical behavior. The Golden Rule can be traced back to several religious and philosophical traditions. For instance, in the Bible, Matthew 7:12 states, "*So in everything, do to others what you would have them do to you, for this sums up the Law and the Prophets*" (NIV). In the context of my upbringing, this principle was hammered into us as the cornerstone of moral conduct. However, my interpretation of the Golden Rule was somewhat skewed. I believed that if I treated others with kindness and respect, they would naturally reciprocate in the same way.

This principle, while noble, doesn't account for the complexities of human behavior. People are influenced by their circumstances, upbringing, and personal struggles, and their responses may not always align with our expectations.

Similarly, the story of the Good Samaritan from the Bible teaches about compassion and helping those in need. In this parable, a Samaritan helps a man who has been beaten and left for dead, while others pass by without offering assistance. The lesson here is to show mercy and kindness to everyone, regardless of their background or situation. The parable, found in Luke 10:25-37, was often cited in school to encourage us to be selfless and compassionate. While this story is a powerful reminder of the importance of compassion, it doesn't suggest that we should neglect our own needs or allow ourselves to be taken advantage of. It's about balance — helping others while also taking care of ourselves.

Early Lessons and Misinterpretations

From the time I was a young kid in Catholic school, I learned that you need to say yes, be supportive, and be helpful. I also grew up with the concept that we didn't say no to a request for help.

Golden Rule Misinterpretation: My understanding of the Golden Rule led me to believe that kindness would always be reciprocated, which is not always the case.

Good Samaritan Influence: The story encouraged me to help others selflessly, but without guidance on maintaining personal boundaries.

It seems like a strange topic to discuss boundaries in terms of forgiveness, but of course, we know that forgiveness is for us personally, not for the other person. Why is that so important? Well, if you are constantly carrying around frustration and anger and not forgiving somebody for their harm to you or their betrayal, then you're the one who's suffering. I've heard it said for years that not forgiving somebody is like drinking poison in hopes that the other person will be harmed, but you're the one drinking the poison.

Resentment and the Importance of Boundaries

So why are boundaries so important in the story of forgiveness? I think it comes down to resentment. When you are always helping other people and wanting to achieve their goals or say yes to someone who needs help, but you're not asking for help, or you're not saying no and setting any boundaries, then you become resentful because you are always doing for others, and it isn't necessarily reciprocated.

That was a hard lesson for me to learn, and it was learned just a couple of years ago. I was under the impression that if I cared for other people or helped other people, then naturally they would reciprocate. I never set any boundaries. I just helped people freely with the false belief that people would help me, love me, and care about me in return.

It's been a hard lesson over the last couple of years to find out that that is not the case. People don't love you because you love them. People don't help you because you help them.

Resentment Builds: Without boundaries, constant helping leads to resentment when help is not reciprocated.

False Beliefs: I believed help and love would be naturally reciprocated, which often is not the case.

That was what I had always believed. That was not what I experienced. So, I've had to learn to set boundaries. I've had to learn to say no. Someone might ask you to do something for them — help them move, give them a call as a reminder, or look something up. But sometimes you have to say no because it isn't suitable for your time frame. You don't have the time, you don't have the energy, or the resources. Benjamin Franklin always said, *"Neither a borrower nor a lender be."* I didn't understand that it had nothing to do with, "getting the money back". It has to do with setting boundaries and taking care of yourself.

Benjamin Franklin's Wisdom

Benjamin Franklin's advice, *"Neither a borrower nor a lender be,"* is often cited to emphasize the importance of financial independence and the complications that can arise from financial entanglements with friends or family. However, it also underscores a broader principle about maintaining clear boundaries to preserve relationships and personal integrity. Franklin's wisdom suggests that entangling oneself in others' affairs — whether financial or emotional — without clear boundaries can lead to complications and resentment.

Franklin's Advice: *"Neither a borrower nor a lender be"* emphasizes the importance of clear boundaries to avoid complications and maintain integrity.

Application: This principle can be applied to emotional and personal boundaries as well as financial ones.

I know this conversation is all about forgiveness. But to me, forgiveness and boundaries go hand in glove. If we set boundaries with other people and learn to say no, or "I can't do that," or "I'll try," or "No, that wouldn't be good for me," then we don't get into that cycle of resentment and anger. My personal story of forgiving someone for my own peace of mind and well-being is so personal that it's been painful for me to even think about, much less write about.

Personal Stories of Forgiveness and Boundaries

The details of the story are not necessary. What is most important is focusing on things like forgiveness. For the last couple of years, I have been focusing on forgiving someone in my life who I am very close to. And what I've learned is, I'm not sure that I'm forgiving the other person or myself for standing by and being the whipping post or being the doormat.

Am I forgiving that person, or am I really forgiving myself? That's the ultimate question on my journey to self-discovery and how to forgive someone who has hurt you and betrayed you so deeply. I've learned to do a lot of research, a lot of reading, and a lot of thinking, and I've created several checklists that allow me to take better care of myself.

Key Lessons Learned

Forgiveness and Boundaries: Setting boundaries helps prevent the buildup of resentment and anger, making forgiveness easier.

Self-Discovery: Forgiving others is intertwined with forgiving oneself for past mistakes and perceived weaknesses.

Research and Tools: Utilizing research and checklists can help in managing emotions and maintaining healthy boundaries.

A big lesson that I've learned recently is that in this life, just because you love someone or care about them, it doesn't mean that they'll care for you. If you show them kindness, their children kindness, or their business kindness, it does not mean that they will like you or that they will be kind to you in return. Somewhere along the line, I got the misinformation that being kind to people meant that they would reciprocate.

If I loved someone, they would love me back, period. If I showed them kindness, gave them love, or was nice to them, then they would do the same back to me. It seems to be a warped sense of the Golden Rule.

It's as if I misunderstood what the Golden Rule meant and thought, "Oh good, if I'm loving to someone and treat them the way I want to be treated, they'll automatically treat me lovingly and be kind to me too." But in the real world, that's not how things work.

All too often, I've been put in a situation where I've been kind to people, and they've been underhanded, sneaky, or disingenuous. It might explain why I've been divorced twice.

Practical Examples and Anecdotes

Workplace Example: At one point in my career, I took on extra projects to help out colleagues, expecting that my generosity would be acknowledged and reciprocated. Instead,

I found myself overwhelmed with work and received little support in return. This taught me the importance of setting clear boundaries and not overcommitting.

Family Dynamics: In family situations, I've often been the one to organize gatherings, help with logistics, and provide emotional support. However, when I needed help, the same energy was not always reciprocated. This imbalance led to feelings of frustration and resentment until I learned to set boundaries and communicate my needs more effectively.

Ultimately, this people-pleasing and this misinformation about being responsible for other people or being kind to people and expecting they'll be kind back has resulted in me putting myself in many awkward positions without these boundaries.

And with this lack of understanding, I've been placed in situations where I've been taken advantage of, or I was thought to be naive, gullible, or easy to get one over on.

So, forgiving those people is really important — not harboring any resentment or anger, but at the same time, I have to work on not being angry at myself and forgiving myself for all of these unfortunate situations.

It seems to me that yes, I don't want to carry around that anger toward someone else because it's venomous. It's poisonous to carry around this anger and animosity. And yes, that won't relieve a lot of the anguish that I'm feeling toward other people.

And of course, I guess I could be angry at the people who inadvertently taught me this, but is it the teacher that taught me this information or just my lack of understanding and immaturity that led me to believe these falsehoods?

Steps Toward Healing and Forgiveness

Writing Letters: One powerful method I learned from my parents, who dealt with their own struggles of forgiveness, is writing letters to the people who hurt you. This allows you to express your feelings fully, even if you never send the letters. My parents wrote letters to their fathers, detailing the pain caused by their addictions. They then read the letters aloud and burned them, symbolically releasing their anger and finding closure.

Professional Guidance: Seeking therapy or counseling can provide new perspectives and tools for managing emotions and setting boundaries.

Mindfulness Practices: Incorporating mindfulness practices like meditation and journaling can help in processing emotions and maintaining mental clarity.

So, I am left with this: it is better to forgive for my own peace of mind, my own sanity, my own growth, and personal well-being than it is to harbor these angry feelings toward people who may not even know that they've hurt me or have hurt me intentionally and don't have any remorse?

It is unnecessary for me to go and ask for their apology? It is only important for me to forgive them so that I can move on with my life and be a better person and love the people in my life more deeply? My family has a lot of addictions, and fortunately for me, my parents were not addicts, but both of their fathers were.

When their father died, what they learned is that they could forgive them by writing a letter, saying everything that needed to be said, reading it out loud, and then burning the letter. Although my grandfathers would never directly hear those messages that had harmed my parents from their youth, my mom and dad were both healed by the act of writing it all down, getting it all out of their system, reading it, and then burning it.

Practical Strategies for Setting Boundaries and Forgiveness

Identify Your Limits: Clearly define what you are comfortable with and what your limits are. This applies to time, energy, and emotional capacity.

Communicate Clearly: When someone asks for your help, be honest about what you can and cannot do. Use statements like, "I can help with this part, but not that" or "I don't have the capacity to help right now."

Practice Saying No: It's okay to decline requests. Practice saying no in a way that is firm yet polite. For example, "I appreciate you thinking of me, but I won't be able to help this time."

Seek Support: Surround yourself with people who respect your boundaries and encourage your growth. This can include friends, family, and professionals like therapists.

Self-Care: Prioritize activities that recharge you and bring you joy. This can help maintain your emotional well-being and make it easier to set and enforce boundaries.

I think my next step on this journey is to do the same thing my parents did. I'm grateful for their open-mindedness and for their ability to share with me ways to forgive and move on with my life. I figured by the time I was 55, I would have it all together. I would have everything all figured out, but it seems like I'm at the beginning and just learning what I need to do to be a better person and take it to the next chapter of my life in a happier, healthier way.

Reflections and Moving Forward

In reflecting on my journey, I realize that setting boundaries and practicing forgiveness are ongoing processes that require constant attention and adjustment. They are skills that can be developed and refined over time, leading to healthier relationships and a more balanced life.

Continuous Learning: Embrace the idea that personal growth is a lifelong journey. Each experience provides an opportunity to learn and improve.

Celebrate Progress: Acknowledge and celebrate the progress you've made in setting boundaries and practicing forgiveness, no matter how small.

Future Goals: Set clear goals for how you want to continue growing in these areas. This could include seeking further education, engaging in self-reflection, or connecting with supportive communities.

By setting boundaries, I protect my well-being and create space for healthier relationships. By practicing forgiveness, I release the burden of past hurts and move forward with greater peace and resilience.

These intertwined practices have transformed my approach to life, enabling me to be a better person, entrepreneur, and loved one. My journey is far from over, but I am committed to continuing to learn, grow, and forgive — both others and myself.

Julia Flynn Werre

Julia Flynn Werre, renowned for her dynamic leadership and strategic acumen in network marketing, pioneers a revolutionary system that propels businesses forward in mere 15-minute intervals.

As the driving force behind onboarding training and content creation at APLGO, she ignites explosive growth, positioning herself as a catalyst for success in the industry.

Julia's expertise extends beyond conventional strategies, transcending limitations to redefine business paradigms. Her approach encompasses a fusion of innovation and practicality, ensuring businesses not only thrive but also sustainably evolve.

From pioneering simple success systems to orchestrating comprehensive business revaluations, Julia's commitment to empowering entrepreneurs is unwavering.

Unleash your business's latent potential with Julia Flynn Werre. Embark on a journey of transformation where strategic insights and actionable steps converge to redefine success.

Contact Julia today and embark on the path to unparalleled growth and prosperity.

CONTACT

Julia Flynn Werre

410-978-8555

http://juliaflynnwerre.com

I WANT TO FORGIVE BUT HOW?

Michael LeBlanc MSW, LCSW

"You need to forgive them." Has anyone ever given you this advice? Five simple words, *"You need to forgive them."*

I had a horrific boss once and that experience filled me with anger, hatred, and rage. It was consuming. I mean daily and multiple times a day, I was consumed with anger and hatred towards him. I remember it felt toxic and, on some level, I knew it was harmful to me — not to him but to me. That's when I knew I needed to forgive him because it was hurting me. *"You need to forgive him."* I hear those five words again.

BUT HOW!? How the heck do you do that when you have so much anger and hatred towards someone? That's the story I want to share with you. I want you to know 'how' so that when you are ready to, you know what to do. I say when you are ready to, because you might not be ready to, and that is okay. But don't live in hatred and resentment too long. Honour yourself and forgive when its right for you.

I shared the story below in my book, *Manifest a Better Life with God: Use Your inherent God Nature* which includes the Law of Attraction, to explain 'how' to forgive. Learn how to shift your anger and heart and energy. In the book, you enter into prayer time with me and God. We are having a conversation on various aspects of how to manifest the life I want. So read below and join in our conversation. Listen to 'how' I forgave and shifted myself out of anger, and hatred to genuinely wanting good for him. Oh, and I'll share the miracle that happened after.

"Remember your worst boss, whom you hated?" God asks.

"Sure, it's easy to remember him; it was an awful experience."

"Remember how you were filled with anger and hatred for a while, and you literally began to feel it having an effect on you?" God asks.

"I do remember feeling as though continuing to be angry and hating him was toxic for me. For months, I constantly had fights with him in my head."

"I want you to think about what you did to change that."

"Well, I remember I was reading this great book called *My Grandfather's Blessings* by Rachel Naomi Remen, and it inspired me to begin to bless him each and every time I thought of him. I did this literally each time, "I tell God.

"I remember journaling often, and other times just blessing him in my head. Literally, anytime the anger and hate would build up, I'd stop myself and picture him, and wish for him all the good things I wished for myself. I remember too that I worked to genuinely feel this from my heart and to want these things for him. I tried to feel it and not just say the words."

"And as you shifted your focus and thinking to something that was more in alignment with your inherent nature, do you remember what that did?" God asks.

"I do; I remember that I began to genuinely feel a bit less anger and hate and actually shifted to a place where I really did want good things for him. It didn't feel like that at first, but it did shift to that."

"And what I really remember," I say, excited again, "is that after doing this for about two weeks, I got a brand-new boss whom I loved, and that was absolutely fantastic, a miracle really!"

"*Perfect,*" God says. "*You initially got caught up in the negative life experience you were having. You had your focus set on all the reasons you hated the guy, so your emotions were negative and intense because your focus was very much not aligned with your inherent God nature, which does not hate. You were set on anger and hate for quite a while. By the law of consciousness, law of attraction, more conditions that were negative continued. Do you recall that?*"

"Yes; I kept having more negative experiences and bad interactions with him. It was pretty awful."

God continues, "*But when you deliberately shifted to thinking and seeing yourself giving love, good, and blessings to him you were shifting your focus to be in alignment with the God within you. You in turn felt better. You deliberately shifted your consciousness and vibrational state and, by law, you received love, good, and a blessing in the form of a new and improved boss.* "

"*When we began, I said you are always dealing with consciousness and not conditions. By deliberately changing your thinking and consciousness about your boss by blessing him, you shifted how you felt; you shifted your vibration, and the law of consciousness, law of attraction shifted the condition for you. You did all of that by deciding to shift your focus and attention and thinking.*"

Shift consciousness, and the conditions will take care of themselves because of the law of consciousness, and the law of attraction."

"Do you not see that in this Consciousness, there is no other Presence to act, except what you are conscious of?" Godfré Ray King, *The I AM Discourses.*

"So, when I was focused on everything I disliked about my boss and his actions I felt anger and hate, negative emotions, because this focus was not aligned with what my inherent God nature knows to be true. Is that correct?" I ask.

"Yes; your focus was on all things you did not like or want, and the 'offness' of this registered as negative emotions," God replies.

"And then when I began to shift my focus and bless him and want only good for him this was more aligned with my inherent God nature, and therefore I began to feel relief and better and more positive emotions."

"Exactly," God says. *"And of course, the law of consciousness, law of attraction responded to both, its law."*

"Thy will be done on earth as it is in heaven," I say to God.

He smiles and looks at me. *"What about it?"*

"It is a part of scripture, a quote I have heard throughout my life. If I think of 'heaven' as pure God consciousness and us as being expressions of you then there is already heaven on earth. We, as people and nature, are heaven on earth. The dramas in life are simply us distorting heaven on earth, but when we bless life, self or others and do so more and more instead of cursing it or complaining, we allow more and more of heaven on earth."

"In the book I referred to earlier, *The Hidden Gospel,* Neil Douglas-Klotz offered a few translations of 'Thy will be done on earth as it is in heaven.' I find them fitting with all you have been sharing with me:"

"Let your delight flow through us, in wave and particle."

"Let your pleasure manifest in us, in light and form."

"Each of you has more influence in life than you realize just by blessing life," God says.

Michael LeBlanc

Michael has over 34 years of experience helping others align with their Divine Intelligence, gain clarity, embody their dream fulfilled and take inspired action, all to manifest their best life. He is an Amazon Best Selling Author (x3), Licensed Clinical Social Worker, Certified Coach, Certified Reiki Practitioner and International Corporate Trainer.

He specializes in creating custom guided meditations for stress, wellness and manifesting. He has designed and delivered trainings worldwide for corporations like Chevron, ExxonMobil, Teck, Corning Inc, Saudi Aramco to name a few. He also has an online store and designs inspirational gifts using his garden photography.

Email: Michael@ManifestwithMichael.com or Michael@DivineDirt.net

Website: ManifestwithMichael.com and DivineDirt.net

LinkedIn: Michael LeBlanc MSW, LCSW.

www.linkedin.com/in/manifestwithmichael

YouTube: ManifestwithMichael

Facebook:
https://www.facebook.com/createwithconsciousness

Instagram: ManifestwithMichael

THE WAY TO HEALING

Josef Stetter

Our ideas, behaviours, and relationships are all influenced by the trauma or meaning that we add to our experiences as children, which casts a long shadow over our lives. The wounds that we sustain throughout our formative years, whether they are the result of emotional neglect, physical abuse, or psychological agony, frequently remain unhealed and have an impact on how we navigate the world. Oh, the scars we carry from our childhood! Whether it's from being ignored, getting roughed up, or going through mental torment, those wounds tend to stick with us and shape how we go about life.

Some of the experiences that can be misinterpreted as major but are actually small and happen to everyone at least once might include: being rejected by your first crush, being yelled at for decorating the walls with your creative expressions of art, watching and listening to parents argue, failing a test, missing a shot, may end up stopping us from trying to achieve success and stepping into our greatness.

Others can be more detrimental experiences like being severely bullied and called names, suffering from neglect, experiencing racism and more! Sadly, the list is endless and over time creates a pattern of insecurity and fear that ensures we keep playing small.

I always joke that some people have issues, well I have a subscription with memories or experiences that are collectible.

The fact is, I experienced many of the items listed above and a few others that impacted my life for many years as I did not understand how to forgive myself and others to move forward and step into the light of who I really am.

The journey toward healing, on the other hand, is totally doable and crucial; if we want to boost our self-esteem and unlock our awesome potential. Get ready for some practical measures to forgive yourself and the person who caused the trauma and open yourself to your true purpose and gifts.

Let's dive in! This will open a whole new world of personal growth, triumph, and the chase for the wildest dreams that stem from passion and purpose.

1. Yes, we see what's going on here and we're totally cool with it. But hey, before you dive into the whole forgiving thing, it's important to acknowledge and come to terms with the fact that you went through something intense. The fact is that both as a child and as an adult you interpret an event, have a particular listening, or remember something a certain way.

We all do this and for many of us, we do not even realize we are using filters to create our experience of life. I remember a promise my father made to come see me in a sporting event and he could not come as he had to work. As a child, we do not understand this concept and in our mind, we draw conclusions such as dad does not care or does not love me. As a 3–6-year-old you were embarrassed when you peed your pants and others might have laughed or reacted in the moment and all you wanted to do was crawl under a rock.

These cause trauma that impacts us more than we know and when we realize it happens to everyone there is some sense of 'it's not that bad.'

Bob Marley was once asked if there is a perfect woman to which he replied: *"Who cares about perfection?"* Even the moon is not perfect, it is full of craters. The sea is incredibly beautiful, but salty and dark in the depths. The sky is always infinite, but often cloudy.

So, everything that is beautiful isn't perfect, it's special to someone. Stop being "perfect", but try to be free and live, doing what you love, not wanting to impress others! Therefore, every human refusing to acknowledge or accept the pain only drags it out, making it harder for us to bounce back.

When we confront our past head-on, with a healthy dose of courage and honesty, we gain the power to reclaim control of our lives and call the shots. You can address one issue at a time and at whatever pace you need so that you can move forward and achieve the legacy you were put on this earth to do.

Picture this: someone who survived the rollercoaster ride of childhood emotional abuse, only to spend years brushing it off like it was no big deal. They finally grasp the impact of their past and accept that the whole traumatic ordeal wasn't their doing, thanks to therapy or some serious soul-searching.

So, you want to break free, huh? Well, the first thing you've got to do is face the music, my friend.

2. Forgiving oneself with a touch of compassion.

Recovering from childhood trauma can be quite a journey, and let's be honest, forgiving oneself can be a real doozy. But hey, it's also the most transformative part of the whole process. So, buckle up and get ready for some serious self-forgiving shenanigans!

Survivors, bless their hearts, sometimes end up carrying around this unnecessary burden of blame and shame. This can also lead to generational trauma which can be even more detrimental and difficult to break the chains of misery and self-inflicted limitations. It's like they've convinced themselves that they don't deserve any love or happiness. Can you believe that? Ridiculous!

There is someone for everyone, you just need to keep trying until the right person at the right time comes into your life! If you have seen the show *American Pickers* where they visit individuals that hoard and collect a wide variety of things many are happily married. Even Sheldon from *Big Bang Theory* with all his quirks found the right match for him.

I have been rejected more times than I can remember. I have dated women from one month to a year and still could not find the ONE, but I kept on trying and learning from every experience.

It took me a long time to meet my Soulmate and I only got married at age 42. Now, five years later, we have an amazing and beautiful relationship, and my wife has gifted me with two incredible children.

Practicing self-compassion is a must if you want to escape this never-ending cycle. So, here's a fun little exercise for you: write a letter to yourself, but instead of gushing about how amazing you are, acknowledge those little faults and mistakes you've made in the past. If you don't, you might fall into the trap of always seeking perfection from yourself and from others which is a one day some day in the future that never happens.

It's like giving yourself a big ol' warm hug of understanding and forgiveness. For instance, a person who has survived the experience of being neglected as a child can write, *"I can't believe I actually thought I was unlovable. Talk about a wild imagination!"*

Alright, so here's the deal. I was just a little kid, you know? And as a kid, I deserved to be taken care of and loved. So, I'm not going to beat myself up over it. No guilt here! People can boost their self-worth and pave the way for inner peace by indulging in some self-forgiveness.

It's all about giving yourself a break and letting go of past mistakes. After all, it's called the human experience not Barbie land. We all have versions of being challenged, getting knocked down, failing but persevering and continuing to be determined that makes us come out on the other side stronger and better.

3. So, here's the deal: forgiving the person who messed you up doesn't mean you have to become best buddies or start making excuses for their behaviour.

Nope, not at all. Letting go of grudges and taking charge of our own story are the key ingredients here. Let's face it, trying to empathize with someone who committed a crime is no walk in the park. But hey, it can make this whole process a little less painful. To get this done, you don't have to give them a thumbs up for their behaviour. Just remember that even people who are hurt can end up hurting others.

It's all part of being human, I guess. I remember having kids calling me names like fat, stupid and many others as I also experienced racism, only to bump into the individuals many years later and sharing with them how they traumatized me and to have them apologize to me for simply being immature kids that did not know better. We weren't best friends after the apology, but I felt empowered and ready to step into SUCCESS.

Now picture them having a mind-blowing epiphany: their abuser was once a victim too! It's like a never-ending loop of misery and dysfunction that has plagued their entire existence. Crazy, right? When people start seeing things from a more empathetic perspective, they can untangle the messy knot of anger and resentment. This frees them up to build healthy relationships and chase after their own passions.

4. "Boundaries and Self-Care:"

After going through some seriously messed up stuff, it's super important to set some boundaries to keep yourself sane and feel safe again. Well, if you want to survive in this crazy world, you might want to consider avoiding those toxic people, standing up for yourself, and making self-care your number one priority. Just saying.

For the sake of their sanity, someone who has survived a rough childhood might decide to set some ground rules with certain family members who just can't seem to stop causing trouble for everyone involved. Yes, it might be hard to set some boundaries as we are creatures of habit but stay firm to your values and beliefs and in the long run people will respect the boundaries that were set.

I have had to choose to stop speaking to family members for long periods on end for them to understand that the boundaries MUST be respected. People can create some serious room for healing and growth when they respect these limits. It's like giving yourself permission to focus on your passions without being weighed down by all that past baggage. Pretty cool, huh?

5. So, here's the deal: if you want to break free from the chains of childhood trauma, you got to embrace your inner badass and find something that gives your life meaning.

It's all about developing that tough-as-nails attitude and finding your true calling. You must find your passion and purpose, God, Creator, the light or whatever higher power you believe in put you on this earth for a reason. It is your job to continue growing until you realize your true calling and leave your mark on earth. Turning life's lemons into lemonade and using heartache as fuel for meaningful change are both crucial parts of this journey.

Take someone who's been through a childhood full of ebbs and flows. Instead of letting it bring them down, they use their experiences to help others going through the same thing. Talk about turning lemons into lemonade! People really take charge of their lives when they start following their passions and principles. And you know what? It's contagious! They inspire others to embark on their own journeys of healing and self-discovery.

Final thoughts:

Even though childhood traumas can leave lasting marks on our minds, they don't have to dictate our destiny. So, picture this: we break free from the chains of our past and set off on a wild journey of healing and self-discovery. How? By tapping into the incredible superpower of forgiveness.

Yes, forgiving ourselves and others can be a total game-changer. By embracing self-compassion, empathy, boundaries, and resilience, we can break free from our past and pave the way to a successful and fulfilling future.

It's like building a bridge to happiness! As we stumble along this crazy road, let's not forget that healing is like a rollercoaster ride, unpredictable and full of twists and turns. But hey, with a little bit of courage, determination, and a helping hand, we can always find our way back to feeling better.

Visualize and implement what your life looks like when you have waved that magical wand and stepped into your greatness. DREAM IT, IMAGINE IT, Describe it with every one of your senses and in vivid details. Share the experiences you are having and the impact you are making to make this world a better place. How amazing is that!

Josef Stetter

For over 18 years, Josef Stetter has incorporated humour, energy, passion and full self-expression into his personal and professional life.

- Award Winning and International Best-Selling Author of 11 books.

- Award Winning Speaker and Guinness World Record participant

- Did not know what he wanted to do when he grew up so switched careers nine times and jobs 18 times

- Worked in Recruitment. Clients have included: Deloitte & Touche, Aecon Construction, Tata Consulting Services, Canon, Aviva, Skechers Shoes and more!

- Personally, helped over 12,000 find a job they love with a 90% success rate of finding anyone employment in any field in under 3 months with proven systems. Fastest he helped people land their dream job now is two days.

- Josef Stetter brings forth an interesting twist to getting things done and achieving results that go well beyond expectations.

- Josef Stetter helps you take the headache out of navigating the abyss of job searching or hiring by sharing advanced strategies that maximize results. He understands the importance of clear, concise, confident, and conversational communication to generate results that are truly unbelievable!!

Contact Information:

https://josefstetter.com/ or joe@celebrategroup.ca
https://www.linkedin.com/in/josefstetter/

KNOWLEDGE IS POWER
FORGIVENESS IS FREEDOM

Patrick Rood

We have all heard the saying that knowledge is power, but I would like to shift your thinking on that aspect for a brief moment. Hopefully my words later on in this chapter will shed some light on why I have turned this phrase into something that to me, and conceivably to those reading this a tool to unlock the power within you and unleash your potential on the world:

Applied knowledge is power. This means that while you can easily attain all sorts of knowledge in this day and age of AI and technology, unless you put that knowledge to use you will never truly possess the power that the knowledge contains.

So, who am I and how can I speak with any authority on this matter? First of all, I am a proud father to three amazing children, but I am also an international best-selling author, speaker, coach, tax strategist, fractional CFO, mentor, real estate investor, financial strategist, Forbes contributor, and lover of life and adventure.

I have also been through my fair share of hell, including the loss of loved ones, bankruptcy, financial ruin, divorce, and some other things, but you aren't here to read about my tales of woe and bad decisions. My main focus in my business has been for many years, working with companies all across the country, helping them lower their tax liability, handling many complex tax situations, and, most of all, helping them grow their business.

I first want to take you through what inspired me to start my business and begin helping people grow their businesses and ultimately accomplish their dreams.

When I was in high school, my father decided to start his own business. He had worked for 30 years in his industry and became one of the best in plastic Extrusion. He had finally gotten to the point where most people also arrived and became entrepreneurs, and that point is when you are tired of making everyone else rich while you struggle to survive.

My father had no college education; he was a self-made man. He had a dream for our family, and the education that he did have was from the School of Hard Knocks in the profession that he was trying to turn into his very own manufacturing business. He had worked with large automakers such as Ford, General Motors, Chrysler, and Hyundai, so they were familiar with some of his work already because of the projects he had worked on during his employment with other manufacturers.

These relationships would have allowed him to start his business from nothing and grow it over six years to a multimillion-dollar enterprise. As most people understand these days, it is vital just to be selective about the people you surround yourself with, and the trust you place in these advisors can be paramount when starting your business.

Some of you may have been told there are three vital components that you need when you're starting your own business. The first is a good banker, the second is a good accountant, and the third is a good lawyer. These are your power players, and these are the people that will help you keep your business in compliance and help you with the most complicated matters, especially when it comes to your business and the government.

I don't know about the banker my father had; to my knowledge, he didn't have a proper accountant, and my father did not particularly trust lawyers. So, in these three aspects, he was sorely lacking. If there had been a better method and someone who was an unbiased third party that could have advised my father about dealing with the IRS in dealing with situations that can sometimes arise when you're late filing returns or when you don't pay your taxes, he would still be in business to this day. But unfortunately, he did not have this third-party advisor that he so desperately needed.

When the IRS did come to him with issues about underpayment and lack of filing returns, he was forced to close his business, sell his equipment to one of his clients and go to work for them while he paid the IRS off.

My parents did all that they knew how to do; they kept good books, they learned QuickBooks, they tried to hire people, but in the end, there was no one that was able to give my parents the advice that they needed to keep their business. So, it went under, and we closed our doors.

I will never forget, as stressful as it was sometimes, the joy that we had and the adventures that we were able to have because my father owned his own business and all the headaches that came along with it.

My father would have to come to work when any of the employees called out and helped run the show. He jumped right in on the line. Sometimes my sister and I would jump right in along with him, but we were still very young, and so there was only so much that we could do in a factory. There were nights when we had slumber parties in the office, sleeping in sleeping bags underneath desks because my father and mother had to work the third shift because someone had shown up drunk or called in sick.

It was a great experience as a young person. We got to see the possibility of what you could build with nothing more than your knowledge and your imagination. It was also a testament to what stress can do to you.

When the business was failing, when the business was just about to close, my father ended up in the hospital having mini-strokes. He nearly had a mild heart attack or near heart attack, I don't remember which, but those were scary times. I remember being worried about what was going to happen to my father and what was going to happen to our future.

I didn't even know half of what was going on. My parents did such a good job protecting us that, yes, we knew my father was sick. We knew my father was having health issues. We didn't know that they were coming from stress, and we didn't know that they were coming from the close of the business. Even when my father was continually losing money, he still paid his employees first, and he made sure that our family never went without.

Because of that, I respect my father as a man, an entrepreneur, and a provider. As most people have issues with their parents growing up, growing up with my father wasn't always easy. He had some anger issues, he never abused me and my sister or my mother, but as a father, now that's one of the things that I try to work on and make sure that my son knows how much I love him, just like my father made sure I knew how much he loved me.

I try to do better than my father and make sure that my son sees his father dealing with his anger in a healthy way and learns to be a better man because of me. Now you may say or be wondering what all of this has to do with the IRS's dirty little secret and what does this all have to do with this book?

Well, the truth is that this all has to do with why I'm writing this book and why I became a tax strategist and fractional CFO. I wanted to give other people the opportunity to succeed in their businesses, which my parents never had. I want to give people the advisor that my parents needed but never had and the opportunity to come in contact with them.

This is why I started my tax practice, became an international award-winning author, and became a Grant Cardone licensee and certified 10X coach and speaker. There are other people out there who can do what I do absolutely, but we are far and few between.

These days just about anybody can file taxes; millions of people do it on their own through TurboTax or another software every single year. There are people who can help with keeping the books or help you keep your QuickBooks. They can help you keep your financials up to date, but there are very few people that know the tax code well enough and know the practical applications; who are also skilled at knowing how to work with the IRS to either avoid situations that can lead to what my father went through.

You need someone who can help you deal with those situations in a way that will keep you in business. That way, you don't have to go through what my family and I did.

It took a long time, but I had to forgive my father's previous accountant and use the experience to fuel my own success and help others not fall victim to the same issues my father faced.

I wanted you to get an idea of who I am, why I do what I do, and why it is my greatest passion. To those of you who know me personally and have heard me say my mission is to screw the IRS out of as much money, LEGALLY, every year as possible. As Dave Ramsey says, *"Millions of people give an interest-free loan to the government every single year needlessly."*

As Grant Cardone says, *"If you aren't operating in some kind of business, you are just giving away money."* So, I invite you, friends, to come on this journey with me to learn how to take control of your finances and learn the dirty little secrets hidden in plain sight that aren't really secrets at all.

It's just that no one has been communicating things plainly the way that I'm going to communicate to you in this book, in a way that's easily digestible and personally applicable to your life, It shows you how to take advantage of what's available to you so that you can set yourself up to win in life and business.

As Robert Kiyosaki says, *"You have to learn the power of cash flow and how it affects your life, business and taxes, and once you understand that you can attain true freedom."* Freedom that comes from forgiveness and knowledge. Freedom born from these two pieces paves the way for a future you can only imagine. Choose to be free my friends, financially free, resentment free, and regret free.

Patrick Rood

Patrick Rood, originally from Jackson, Michigan. is now the owner of Rood Financial Services Tax Strategy and CFO firm. They have three locations currently — one in Michigan, Philadelphia, Pennsylvania and Tampa, Florida they are currently covering clients in over 13 states across the country.

Patrick is a Grant Cardone certified 10X Coach & Speaker, a two-time award-winning international bestseller, and the author of the new book *The IRS Dirty Little Secrets*.

Patrick is a Guinness Book of World Records holder. As a serial entrepreneur having several businesses throughout the years and witnessing many successes and failures from entrepreneurs around the country his passion became helping people succeed in life and business.

He also spent 8 years in university traveling around the country doing volunteer work and educating people through drama and the arts.

He is also the proud father of three beautiful children. His mission is to help individuals and entrepreneurs from a side hustle or start-up to multi-million dollar companies with structure, compliance, and retaining profits.

The goal is to keep more of your hard-earned money in your pocket and make the tax code work for you instead of being taken by the system. Patrick can truly help you leverage the methods and strategies the super-wealthy use to retain generations of financial control and security.

Contact Patrick:

info@roodfinancial.us

THE ACTION OF FORGIVENESS

Anthony T Cutno Jr

Every individual on this planet, from the murderer serving a quadruple life sentence in prison to our pet wants to be forgiven for whatever reason. Forgiveness is an action just like the action that was done by the individuals that I must forgive.

This action is a powerful and extremely hard act to accomplish. I can say I forgive but do I really forgive? We never forget the act that was done, the words said to even be capable to contemplate the action of forgiveness. We all know the saying I forgive you, but I won't forget. That alone is really saying I will not forgive you; I'll just hold on to it for later.

To truly perform the act of real forgiveness is a very personal and empowering action; it must be a choice to sincerely forgive and forget. I must release negative emotions, then choose to keep these individuals in my life or allow myself and them to move on with life like nothing happened.

This is the true act of forgiveness, no matter what was done and said, I must forgive and forget. I along with every induvial on the planet must release ourselves from the chokehold of pain, pettiness, anger, resentment and bitterness. Forgiveness is a spiritual and physical gift we must give ourselves; it is not for the individual that wronged us.

I am going through this currently in my personal life, have been for about two years now. I also suffer from internal medical issues that affect me physically that you won't know unless I tell you, from my time in the Marine Corps.

Since I started on my mental and spiritual healing journey, I can honestly say I discovered His purpose for me. The forgiveness side of this journey is extremely hard especially when you must see these people on a regular basis, even harder if these are family members.

Myself, I have found that since starting to talk with the Lord, living what I speak, I am walking in my purpose. True forgiveness is not hard to do when we genuinely say, "*I forgive you*", if they apologize to me. The same must be done when I speak the words, "*I accept your apology*".

Now on the other side of that action, is the individual whose apology I am accepting, along with the individual I am forgiving. What they do after that is not either my or your concern. The true act of forgiveness is biblical and must be taken seriously on both sides of that action, because the reaction to that action will be given to us both come judgment day when our life is being reviewed from the Great Book.

Then the Lord will either say he doesn't know us, leave his presence, or Enter into the joy of thy Lord. If he doesn't allow karma to do her job, I already received and lived my karma. This is why forgiveness is for me not them.

It also has a few life benefits, due to me forgiving and not holding on to all that pain, hurt, and resentment from not truly forgiving and just letting it go. I could never really move on, however once I started to truly heal and forgive, I started to heal in multiple ways inside and out.

I slowly stopped being angry a lot, easily triggered, more talkative and friendly. This came from healing emotionally and mentally on the inside. I started learning my true self, I started to understand myself, which allowed me to understand others, and this led me to self-awareness, which allowed it to show it on the outside.

Through this process along with my own spiritual belief, I began the forgiveness process to help me heal emotional wounds that were still open, many I didn't know were open. This brought me true clarity not only emotionally but also inner peace. Matthew 6:14 says, *"For if you forgive other people when they sin against you, your heavenly Father will also forgive you."*

areThis is why forgiveness is for me not them. It allowed me to release the emotional baggage, that I didn't know was stopping me and more than likely doing the same to you reading these words. Inner peace and emotional well-being are what you are or will be eventually missing. You probably just realized it.

Family and friends are very important to me just as they are to every person and other animal species on the planet. Family is not always blood or the same species for that matter, we all have, had, and will have conflict with these individuals at some point in any relationship.

Even the Lord had issues within his circle, and he forgave them in the end and moved on with his life purpose. I and we must do the same. Aren't we after all made in his image and he gave us all the power of choice and free will?

Forgiving others can most likely improve, if not, it can fix a relationship. It only takes one person to start the forgiveness process, however it must be more than one person in the process. Proper communication must be achieved. Although for whatever reason proper communication doesn't happen, the action of true forgiveness must still occur.

This is done through prayer, just saying the Lord knows what's in my heart, blah blah will not get the job done. This is defying the Lord and holding onto that anger, pain, hurt, resentment and just being petty. Tell the God that you pray to that your prayer is to forgive that person and then speak the words, "*I forgive them Lord*," these words must be meant when spoken.

Another benefit of being able to truly forgive is that it shows not only yourself but others that you have grown as a person. Personal Growth is a positive reaction to forgiveness.

Once. I started to recognize what was happening to me, I was able to use this new tool and power as a dynamic tool and shield, to help me grow into the new man I am becoming. It allows me to learn from past experiences, develop new skills, open new doors for the new person I am becoming and cultivate resilience due to me just not worrying about what was done to me, who did it and why.

Learning to forgive allowed me and will allow you, the reader, to simply do the same. Eliminate the wanting to know the WHY effect. Once I found the WHY, it was allowed to become irrelevant, why this person did this to me, that to me, why this person said this, why, why, and why.

Since I was not getting the why, I was just getting excuses, or it was flipped to be my fault. Then came the WHY. Why they won't take accountability, why they can't see what they did and the result of what they did. Why I am still suffering because of what they did.

Wanting to know the reason for all these WHY's will stress you out, then you will also be suffering from that stress. The stress had me homeless and killed me a few times. This is why forgiveness is for me not them.

Spiritual forgiveness is a deeper understanding of forgiveness. You must forgive yourself first. I had to forgive myself for allowing those things to happen to me, the betrayal, manipulation, lies, and tricks. Spiritual forgiveness begins with self-forgiveness. I had to acknowledge my part in what happened, had to remind myself that I'm not perfect and karma is real. It's just my turn on karma's schedule. Forgiving yourself is self-compassion and the first move towards self-acceptance and personal growth.

I'll conclude with this; I am still on this journey of fulfilling His purpose for me and I don't know where it is taking me. When it comes to the forgiveness part of my journey, I'm learning that the spiritual and the individual worldly action of forgiveness is not only connected but that it goes hand and hand with the physical, personal and spiritual transformative journey.

You cannot grow in any true form without performing the action of true forgiveness. True forgiveness is finding a path that resonates with your beliefs and allows you to experience greater peace, love, and spiritual growth. This cannot be accomplished without truly forgiving yourself, then others, it is written, it has been spoken. True peace and clarity come from not only forgiveness; however, you cannot receive worldly and spiritual peace and clarity without forgiveness. This is why forgiveness is for me not them.

Anthony T Cutno Jr

Anthony T Cutno Jr, was born on October 22, 1983, in New Orleans LA and was raised between New Orleans and Atlanta GA. He graduated from Redan High School in Stone Mountain GA in 2000 and entered Air Force boot camp in September of 2004. After being kicked out, he joined the Marine Corps a few days later, and went to boot camp in March of 2005, in Parris Island.

Anthony retired from the Marine Corps in June of 2018. He's a motivational, inspirational speaker. Anthony uses himself along with his life as an example to motivate, inspire other men and veterans, turning his traumatic and unique life into motivation for others. He uses those traumatic experiences and changes them into positive motivation to inspire not only them but the world around them through God and pure will power. It is his own way of self-therapy since conventional therapies did nothing.

Contact Anthony:

Devinewarriorsdimension@gmail.com

Devinewarriorsdimension.com

FORGIVENESS RELEASED ME FROM A PRISON OF MY CONFINEMENT

Karen Hewitt

It was a decade; ten years filled with pain, suffering, anxiety, and so much more. I was constantly making the statement that they didn't deserve my forgiveness. They deserved my anger. I didn't realize that this had stopped me from living and loving my life.

You've probably heard the saying, *"Letting them live rent-free in your head."* Well, this person became a squatter who was systematically tearing down every fixture in my mind, fleecing the copper pipes, and just leaving me feeling worthless.

Over 20 years ago, after I had left a loveless marriage that everyone agreed was a mistake from day one, I met and fell head over heels in love with a man from the USA who promised me the whole universe. He was a military man, a churchly man, and a southern gentleman. I moved from the UK to Arizona to be with him, and we were married by the church's Bishop personally in his office. We celebrated with family and friends a few weeks later.

It was a fantastic life. I got a job that quickly developed into a career. For my birthday, he got me a blue-nosed pit bull puppy, whom I named Daisy. This was short for Oops-A-Daisy, as she would break her runs by aiming at a wall. He had told me that he retired from the military shortly before our wedding. He took a little time off from work,

He would drive me to work, bring me lunch, and pick me up. Everyone who met him would either tell me not to tell their wives how he treated me because they would want the same treatment or how they wished their spouse would be more like him. He would open the door for me, but I couldn't carry anything more than a purse, pull out chairs, or surprise me with flowers and my favorite chocolate milkshakes from a diner nearby.

Life was perfect!

He would constantly compliment me on outfits I chose, meals I cooked, or how I would do my hair. He was not a stranger to letting me know how much he loved it when I did certain things. This was still in the beginning.

In hindsight, I see now when it changed from "You look beautiful" to "Why don't you wear the dress from last week that you looked so beautiful in?" He was crafting every single piece of me through positivity. I dressed how he wanted, slowly removed people from my life he didn't like, which included putting up a wall between my family and me. After all, it was so expensive to call England and speak to my Mum; he managed the finances and would let me know when it was possible.

I still never expected that first slap. The apologies came afterward, the tears, the story about his over-controlling father who beat him constantly, and the demons he was fighting. I forgave him; it was supposed to only be one time, and it would never happen again.

Till it happened again, and again, and again.

Each time, it was easy to forgive him, not because I forgave him but because I believed I deserved this treatment. I burned dinner and forgot to do laundry or move it from the washer to the dryer. By the way, many of these simple execution tasks I now know were a product of undiagnosed ADHD.

In my mind, if I could be a better human, wife, or employee, this would all go away. This may be hard for some people to read, but it was just bruises at that point in my journey. Within two years, it turned into a broken bone, a pillow being held over my face, being strangled till I was unconscious. I still cannot wear crew neck shirts or scarves because the feeling of any pressure around my neck causes me to freeze. I endured daily punishment and attempts on my life because I felt I deserved each kick, hit, punch, and utter humiliation that came my way.

Then, one day, he hit me in full view of an assistant manager at my work. I was opening the store, and he dropped me off. When I said something, he felt was disrespectful, I was punished immediately. That person wasn't supposed to be there, but they were and saw it.

Jumping into action, they sat me down and told me I didn't deserve this. They started the escape plan. Organizing this took a couple of days, but he was arrested over a broken taillight, and I had every intention of bailing him out of jail to beg for forgiveness. Forgiveness was a big part of the story; I forgave him for hurting me but asked him to forgive me because I had made him do it. I went to work the next day in tears, feeling broken because I thought that I was the one in the wrong; that I was the one needing to be forgiven.

That day, a kind older gentleman told me something that has shaped my life since then.

He was born in Japan and had immigrated to America; now in his eighties, he made me come next door to a coffee shop for some tea, and I broke down in tears. Telling him how much forgiveness I needed for my actions against the man I was married to, that I was broken.

He told me I wasn't hurt; I was Sakura, the cherry blossom. A tree that, in its winter, loses all its leaves and flowers, and even the bark goes grey. It looks like it has died. This was when the tree dug down deep to gain strength for the upcoming spring. This gave me the strength with friends to file for divorce and an order of protection, and the lawyer convinced me to tell the police what I had gone through.

I sought therapy and was asked why I hadn't left sooner. Again, I was telling myself I deserved every hit and punch, not realizing how much hurt and hatred I was building in my heart and soul. During the divorce, he tried to take my 401K, seek spousal support, and more, but threatened me in court and ended up losing.

The judge reprimanded him, that he was accountable for his actions. When I heard him being held responsible, I started to hate him, realizing the pain and suffering he had put me through. I couldn't forgive him; the scars, both physical, emotional, and mental, caused me to have a complete nervous breakdown.

I ended up on antidepressants and short-term disability and was diagnosed with CPSTD and agoraphobia. Scared to leave my home in case he saw me and finished the job. Even knowing he was in jail for his actions. I feared and hated most men, seeing them all as threats. In my heart, I felt all men wanted to harm me; the fear gripped me to such an extreme I stopped living life.

I did get remarried, but part of that was this fear that I had to have children to fulfill my earthly purpose. I do not regret this or my children. However, for the longest time, leaving my home was a chore. I went to doctor appointments and became a recluse and a shut-in.

My anger created a prison within my own home. I still dressed as he told me, refusing to buy new clothes or treat myself with any respect. I was determined to hang on to my pain. People would say to me that what he did was unforgivable. So, I refused to forgive him, diving deeper and deeper into hatred and anger.

In 2013, after my third child was born, more than 5 years after I escaped, I started personal development and working with a coach. I still wouldn't leave the house, so network marketing became what I needed to make money.

Over the next two years, I worked on leaving the house, meeting people, and understanding my EQ, not just my IQ. In 2016, just after my 4th child was born, my Mum passed suddenly, and I hit rock bottom again. Words she had said after she found out about the abuse circled in my head.

"Maybe you survived because someone else might not have; tell your story and help others." Almost like words from an

angel, my Mum's council rang through my mind day and night, and I realized that holding onto all this pain, hate, and anger was now trapping me. I was unable to grow, unable to enjoy things, and panic attacks were ruling my life. I decided to forgive him. Not to forget because what he did changed who I am today.

The moment I chose forgiveness, the weight lifted. I joined an organization with weekly in-person meetings to learn to communicate more formally. I began to share how it impacted me and how I don't hold any hurt or hatred anymore.

It was a feeling of letting go. To forgive someone who had intentionally wanted to take my life with their own hands was so empowering to me because it took away all his power over me. The power I had let him have for 10 years after he was no longer a part of my life.

Would I change what happened to me? I have a controversial answer. I would still live through those few years of hell and even the self-imposed prison because it really did shape my empathy, my purpose, and my life.

I do, however, think if it hadn't taken losing my Mum to forgive him, I would have had a few more years, I would have been more involved in activities outside the home, and I would have had a fuller life with more happiness.

That decision to forgive him had no bearing on his life. It had a full bearing on my life; I have lived the last few years not looking where he lives, not being afraid to speak to men, having caution, yes, but not the fear I used to experience.

I started to step into who I am because forgiving and releasing that power allowed me to figure out who I was, how I wanted to dress, and even my vibrant pink hair without thinking it would make someone happy. It allowed me to become the person who was stolen from me for 15 years and is now freer than before.

You see, when you don't forgive, you allow them to still control and have rent-free squatter rights in your mind. Forgiveness, not forgetting, means freedom.

It's time to allow yourself that freedom.

Karen Hewitt

Karen Hewitt: Empowering Connections, Building Relationships

Karen Hewitt, born in England and now living in the USA, is a top social media strategist and network marketer. A mom of five as well as the owner of *Blossom To Success*, she balances family and career with ease and a healthy dose of sarcasm.

As a member of the LGBTQIA+ community and a neurodiverse individual, Karen brings a unique perspective to her work.

With a loving and compassionate nature, she fosters authentic connections and builds strong relationships. She advocates against discrimination and hate, believing in kindness and respect for all.

She creates a supportive, inclusive community through her expertise while helping others achieve their goals in social media and network marketing.

Karen also uses her position on the San Diego Human Dignity Foundation to help others.

Contact Karen:

www.BlossomToSuccess.com

FORGIVENESS IS BADASS

Juanita Kapp

Do you know what hurts more than anything in the world? I can sum it up in one word: *Betrayal*! Being betrayed by someone we love dearly has to be one of the most hurtful experiences we can ever have in our lives.

It takes a moment yes, just one moment, to annihilate a lifetime of beautiful memories.

When that moment hits, the moment of betrayal, we feel overwhelmed by disgust at what has just been uncovered. It's that feeling that you get when the truth kicks you right in the stomach. It's the realization that hits when you comprehend that you have been lied to. Have you experienced it before? I have!

Overwhelm, disgust, shock, pain they all come together in that one moment to create a toxic cocktail of shattered dreams and a broken heart.

I have heard the saying *"Ignorance is bliss"* probably a million times in my life. Why am I discussing ignorance right now? There is a very good reason for this: I was ignorant but not only that, I was naïve as well! Instead of my "ignorance" leading to "bliss" it led to a world of uncertainty, second-guessing and disappointment. Yes, I too was a victim of ignorance.

How many times do we choose to ignore the warning signs in a given situation? How many times do we convince ourselves that we are just imagining the unforgiveable? Has that happened to you before? Have you ever loved someone so deeply that you would override your own gut feeling multiple times just to keep that untarnished and polished view of that one special person?

I ask you this: How has your flimsy and unproductive coping mechanisms affected your life and your relationships? Have they brought you to a mental space where you are sound and secure within yourself? Or have they broken down the trust that you have in yourself and who you are? Has mental gymnastics become a part of your daily conflict resolution?

What exactly does mental gymnastics involve? Is it going from one train of thought to the other in the depths of despair while trying to save face and uphold your dignity? Has avoidance been your strategy to emotional survival? It hits deep, it hurts like hell, but it still hits. The truth — it cannot be avoided. It always surfaces in the most unusual ways. Yes, truth: that hard and unforgiving, relentless, and yet magical connection between your language and your thought processes, your mind.

There is so much negativity in this world. So much hurt. So many things that can and do go wrong. People hurting people. People breaking down societal morals and values. Marriages are being destroyed on a daily basis by social media. Murders take place. Wars rage on like there is no tomorrow. Drug abuse is increasing and now affects our younger generation. These are the evils of our current time that we can visibly see.

Is that all that we consciously recognize and feel in our subconscious? Oh no, not at all. On top of all the visible evils there are those even more poignant and stronger evils that destroy us from the inside out. Hate, anger, grief, jealousy, narcissistic behaviour in all kinds of relationships whether it be personal or professional.

The worst of these internal struggles of destruction is something called unforgiveness. You see unforgiveness has its own special, nasty bite. It eats people up from the inside out. It festers, it wounds, and it shapes our reality while quietly suffocating our potential. It's a blinding force of demolition.

When we live our lives with a mindset of unforgiveness it affects everything and everyone around us. Suddenly, all we can see is how we have been wronged. Suddenly, all we think about is how mad we are at the people who hurt us. We feel like they don't deserve our forgiveness because we know, that we know, that we know, that what they did to us was on purpose. Whether that be the case or not, that is how we feel. Let's be honest. More than 90% of us have been through this at one point or another in our lives.

Unforgiveness clouds our judgement, it influences our decision making and it keeps us from living with an open heart. We become closed off to new experiences and potential growth. It breaks down our inner person instead of having that much desired effect on our enemies. It's like stepping in a self-made trap that was constructed to conquer our enemies.

We tell ourselves that unforgiveness will nurture us back to emotional health, but we are lying to ourselves. All unforgiveness does is constrict our freedom. Our negative thoughts and feelings keep us captive and hold us down like a slithering python waiting to devour us and end our existence. Yet, the warmth of the embrace of unforgiveness gives us a false sense of acceptance and love. We believe we are protecting ourselves from the pain by harbouring unforgiveness but the only thing that we are doing is cutting off our own emotional air supply. There is no safety within the confines of our unforgiveness, there is only an abyss of unhappiness and strife. In the end, it brings us to emotional death.

We hold onto unforgiveness because we think that forgiveness is something our perpetrators do not deserve. We think forgiveness is something we give them as a gift that would make them feel better. Something too positive to share with them because in our minds they need to be punished repeatedly. My friend you are so wrong, forgiveness is not for them, it's for you. The only one that is experiencing intense feelings of grief and pain, is most definitely not the one who hurt and betrayed you. They have already moved onto their next victim. They have already forgotten what they have done to you. You are just another notch in their belt.

You have been hurt by these people or situations and now you valiantly continue hurting yourself by living with unforgiveness. Do you know why? Because it's stealing your joy, it's affecting your health in a negative way; it's draining your energy and it's really taking you closer and closer to the edge of misery from which some people never return.

Have you ever felt the need to remove yourself from a person or a situation before? This normally happens right after they have hurt you. That's a natural feeling to have. It's a natural move to make because in essence you are acting in self-preservation. Walking around with unforgiveness raging in your heart and mind, is almost like taking a radioactive piece of that evil act that was committed against you and giving it access to your very heartbeat. That's madness to say the least. It is completely unnecessary and can be handled in a whole different way.

It's time for you to flip the script and focus less on others and more on with working on yourself. You cannot be held accountable for their actions, but you have a choice in what your response is going to be. See, every betrayal and every disappointment as an opportunity to grow and learn more about not only others but about yourself. Sometimes you have to dive into the personal pain in order to discover just how strong and resilient you really are.

I promise you that when you take bold steps to invest in yourself, you are going to be so surprised at what you discover. A whole new journey will open up for you. A whole new chapter of your life will start. Stop going through life just trying to get through your day, that is called existing. Start living! Ditch the unforgiveness, let yourself breathe and put that mindset on repeat every single day.

Get up in the morning and focus on what you are grateful for. Be vocal about it. Scream it to the mountains if you must. You have a responsibility toward the world and most of all yourself to become who you are meant to become. Now ditch the self-pity because that is what unforgiveness stems from. Put on your beautiful personality like a garment of praise. God has blessed you with so many talents. Make that decision today!

Gone are the days of choosing unforgiveness. The python has lost its grip on you. Finally! You are free! You are fabulous! You are enough! Forgiveness is NOT for them, it's for YOU so that you can live a great and amazing life.

Will the doubts come to take you off course? Yes, they will! You have a secret weapon, you have an insurmountable amount of inner strength that only you can wield. You own the day, you own your future. No one can interfere with your destiny if you choose to live with a forgiving and open heart!

Pick up your sword, and be the badass that you were born to be.

Juanita Kapp

Founder & Owner of the *Meticulous Moments Podcast*

Founder & Owner of the *Meticulous Martial Arts Mastermind* Co-Host on *The Joe Cortez: The Happy Hour Show with Joe Cortez*

Co-Founder & Owner of the *KAPPTOR Connection*

Co-Founder of *Business Prowess Podcast*

5 X International Best-Selling Author

Hoinser Media Group Brand Ambassador (Europe)

Global Public Speaker and MC

Spiritual Counselor

Martial Artist (Shorin-Ryu Shorinkan Karate (Kata, Kumite, Bunkai), Self Defence, Wooden and Bladed weapons, Boxing, Kickboxing, Jiu Jiutsu)

UK Black Belt Hall of Famer

Spartan Hall of Warriors President for South Africa

Inducted into the *Action Martial Arts Hall of Honors* in 2024 for Outstanding Achievement in Martial Arts

Executive Producer & Stunt CoordinatorActress

Agent to Shannon *"The Cannon"* Ritch - Hector Camacho Jr, Jarrod Tillinghast

Since she was a young child, she always wanted to *"Tame the pen and the sword"* and has made it her mission to do just that.

She was an ordained Pastor for 15 years and enjoyed working with congregations. She has always been a natural speaker and worked her way up in various Corporations whilst being in the ministry.

In 2020 during the Covid-19 pandemic she decided to change her life and follow her heart's passion. She became an entrepreneur of note through pure willpower and personal choice.

She has since opened various businesses that are highly successful and has started to travel the world. She is excited about the future and the developments that it will present. Personal and Professional development has always been at the top of her priority list.

She travels the globe to share her energy and positive outlook on life with those who cross her path. As an entrepreneur she is a risktaker and will continue to be one. The sky is the limit in what we can achieve, if only we would take the courage to believe.

CONCLUSION

The authors of this book and myself have united to bring you our experiences with the almighty forgiveness. It has taken an unusually long period of time to craft this particular book.

It's always interesting to see which emotions humans have the most around a particular subject. I feel as though God has given me this opportunity to bring people together to write certain books and chapters to share with the rest of the world. Teachings and learnings come in various ways and this book was exceptionally interesting. Authors have come in and out of the book they have rewritten chapters over and over again, including myself. I feel as though we were all exposed to such a volcano of emotions while digging deep into the private energy of our souls.

We are all privileged to present to you our experiences with forgiveness and thank you so much for reading. Forgiveness is always for us not them.

Love and Light

Marianne

FORGIVENESS IS FOR ME NOT THEM